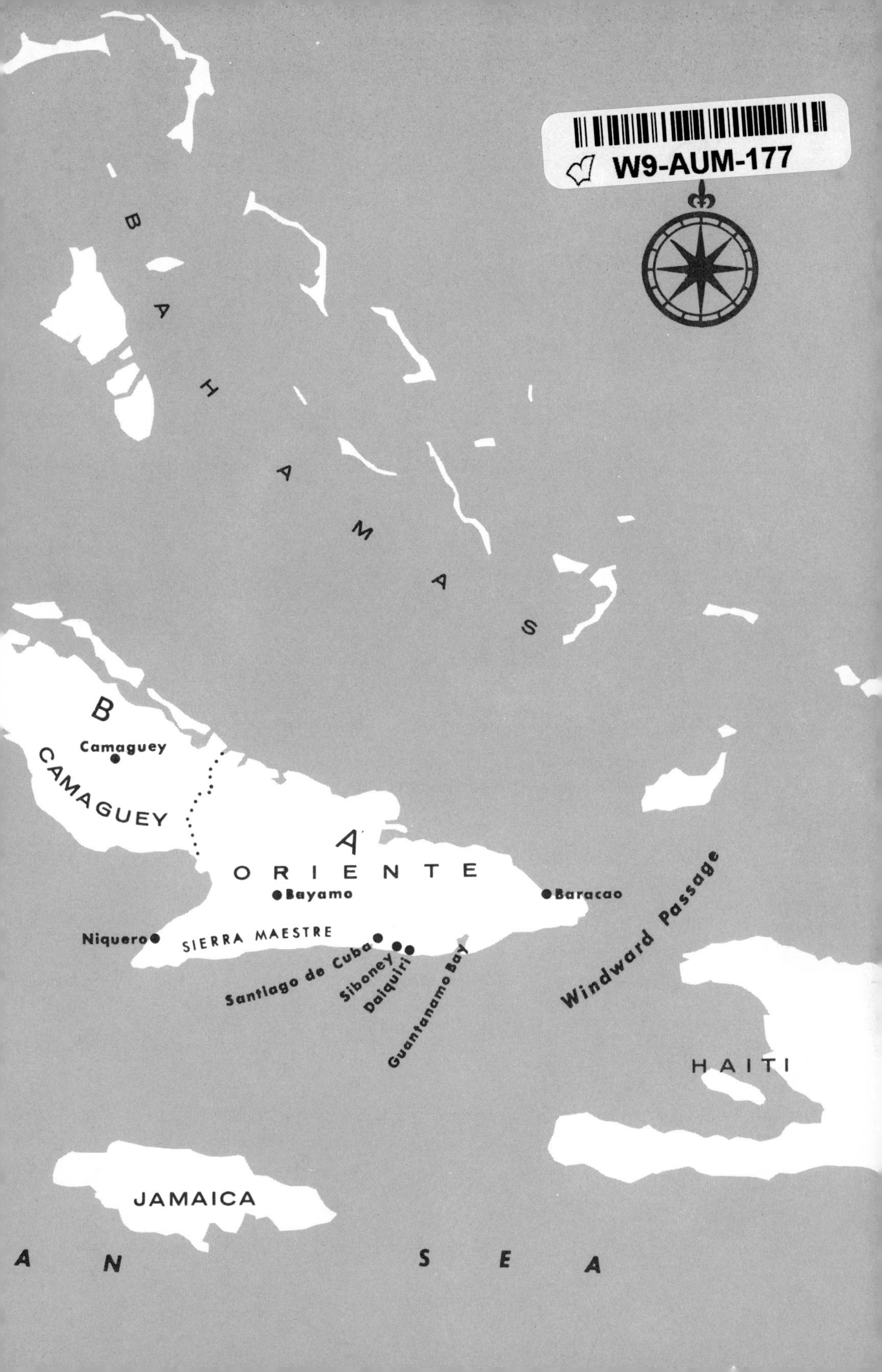

B

A

H

A

M

A

S

B
CAMAGUEY
Camaguey

A
O R I E N T E
Bayamo
Baracao

Niquero
SIERRA MAESTRE
Santiago de Cuba
Siboney
Daiquiri
Guantanamo Bay

Windward Passage

H A I T I

JAMAICA

A N   S E A

The Cuban Revolution

The Cuban

Revolution

BY ROBERT GOLDSTON

DRAWINGS BY DONALD CARRICK

ILLUSTRATED WITH PHOTOGRAPHS

THE BOBBS-MERRILL COMPANY, INC.

INDIANAPOLIS   NEW YORK

photographic research by Lisl Steiner
map by Jack H. Fuller

THE BOBBS-MERRILL COMPANY, INC.
A Subsidiary of Howard W. Sams & Co., Inc.
Publishers INDIANAPOLIS KANSAS CITY NEW YORK

Library of Congress catalog card number: 79-78279
First edition
Designed by Joseph B. Del Valle

For Louise and Frank Novitch

Contents

Six Days in October

October 22, 1962: At 7 P.M. millions of Americans turned on their television sets to hear an address by John Fitzgerald Kennedy, President of the United States. The President's face was grave, his manner grim, his voice sober. As they listened to his precise sentences, his carefully chosen words, the American people suddenly realized that they were face to face with the holocaust of total atomic war.

"This government," said Kennedy, "as promised, has maintained the closest surveillance of the Soviet military buildup on the island of Cuba. Within the past week, unmistakable evidence has established the fact that a series of offensive missile sites is now in preparation on that imprisoned island. . . .

". . . This secret, swift and extraordinary buildup of Communist missiles in an area well known to have a special and historical relationship to the United States and the nations of the Western Hemisphere, in violation of Soviet assurances, and in defiance of American and hemispheric policy . . . is a deliberately provocative and unjustified change in the status quo which cannot be accepted by this country. . . .

John F. Kennedy

". . . Our unswerving objective, therefore, must be to prevent the use of these missiles against this or any other country, and to secure their withdrawal or elimination from the Western Hemisphere. . . ."

The President outlined the basic steps the nation would take in the following days to achieve these objectives. They included continued surveillance through air reconnaissance; a "quarantine" against the delivery of any more rockets or rocket fuel to Cuba; direct though unspecified "action" which could only mean military invasion of the island if the Soviet missile buildup continued; and, finally, all-out atomic war against the Soviet Union if any of the missiles presently located on Cuban soil should be fired at *any* nation of the Western Hemisphere. President Kennedy did not fail to include in his speech a strong plea for a peaceful, rational settlement of the problem. But despite this, to many, perhaps to most, listeners his speech sounded like a scenario for Armageddon.

The Cuban missile crisis was on—and so was the panic. Quite a few Americans—those who could afford it—immediately besieged airline offices booking passage to Mexico, Australia, northern Canada—anywhere out of the country. Many more who could not afford such remote hideouts piled their families into cars and headed for the wide open spaces—anywhere away from the target cities of North America. Thousands of citizens rushed out to their local stores and began stockpiling food and medicines to carry them through the looming catastrophe.

Even while the President spoke, the North American Air Defense had been put on maximum alert; huge bombers of the Strategic Air Command took off to circle through the lonely stratosphere; U.S. ships were taking up their stations around Cuba. And before the President finished speaking all Russian forces were alerted for possible war. There were eighteen Russian dry-cargo vessels, among many others, approaching Cuba at that moment. What would happen when they were stopped, boarded for inspection, and possibly sunk by American warships? There was no precedent in international law for Kennedy's "quarantine." It was a blockade without a war—or, as the Russians hastened to point out, legally, simple piracy. Soviet submarines accompanied some of those freighters; would they stand idly by while hostile forces interfered with their movement? Soviet ground-to-air missiles were stationed in Cuba; would they not be fired at by U.S. reconnaissance planes? A full Soviet division accompanied Russian technicians in Cuba itself; would they not resist any attempted invasion?

October 23: Huge mobs of angry pickets stormed outside U.S. embassies in London, Paris, Rome, and most other capitals of the world protesting the American rush to "the brink" of atomic war—a war which might spell the end of world civilization, possibly even the end of the human race. England's great philosopher Lord Bertrand Russell wired Kennedy: "Your action desperate . . . no conceivable

11

justification." French and English newspapers even questioned whether Russian intermediate- and medium-range ballistic missiles were actually stationed in Cuba. The Soviet government officially rejected the President's "Proclamation of Interdiction of the Delivery of Offensive Weapons to Cuba." Soviet freighters continued on their courses to Cuba.

At the United Nations, American ambassador Adlai Stevenson presented evidence of the Soviet missile buildup in Cuba. Russian United Nations ambassador Valerian Zorin countered that the aerial photos had been manufactured by the Central Intelligence Agency. Stevenson lost his temper. "All right, sir," he cried across the Security Council hall, "let me ask you one simple question: Do you, Ambassador Zorin, deny that the USSR has placed and is placing medium— and intermediate—range missiles and sites in Cuba? Yes or no. Don't wait for the translation! Yes or no!" But Zorin refused to answer.

And in the face of the American air reconnaissance photos any denial would have been useless. It was this fact perhaps which counted most with the governments (as opposed to the people) of America's allies. Messages of official support and solidarity with the U.S. position flowed into Washington from all the North Atlantic Treaty Organization countries and from all members of the Organization of American States.

Civil defense authorities in the southeastern states were alerted; U.S. fighter planes in the area were dispersed lest they present too easy a target. In Florida the largest invasion force gathered since the end of World War II was assembling, while Air Force pilots were briefed on their missions in the event of an air strike against Cuba.

October 24: A letter was received from Soviet Premier Nikita Khrushchev. It was long, rambling, angry and inconclusive. Presidential advisors felt it reflected confusion in the Soviet government. Would the tough Russian leader follow the advice of his own "hawks" or his "doves"? Low-level reconnaissance flights over Cuba (jets screaming in at treetop level) revealed that work on the missile sites was more advanced than had been thought. Two deadly MRBM's were ready to operate.

Nikita Khrushchev

In Moscow, Premier Khrushchev collared a visiting American businessman to proclaim that any conflict in the Caribbean could easily lead to all-out nuclear war, that Russian submarines would sink any American ship forcing a Russian ship to stop. Even while the Soviet leader issued these threats, the President's Security Council in Washington issued orders that any Soviet submarine interfering with the blockade be sunk.

Naval patrol planes reported that sixteen of the eighteen Russian dry-cargo ships heading for Cuba had stopped in their tracks or were circling aimlessly on the high seas. Perhaps, after all, a final confrontation might yet be avoided.

October 25: The Russian vessels turned around. They were returning to the Soviet Union (they would be followed all the way by U.S.

13

reconnaissance planes). But the Russian missiles already in Cuba still posed a threat. Work on their sites was being rushed—more and more of them were becoming operational. Hints of an American invasion of Cuba to dismantle not only the missiles but also the government of Fidel Castro appeared beneath headlines in many American newspapers. U.S. naval forces stopped and boarded a Soviet-chartered Lebanese freighter. When it was found that the ship carried only trucks and truck parts she was permitted to proceed to Cuba.

But what to do about the missiles still in Cuba? The President's Council discussed a program which included the imposition of a complete blockade, increased low-level reconnaissance flights, the dropping of a leaflet addressed to the Cuban people warning them of their peril, a surprise air strike against the Soviet bases, and finally—invasion itself.

October 26: A new letter from Nikita Khrushchev was received in Washington. It was meandering and argumentative. But it suggested that since the Russian missiles were stationed in Cuba only to deter a possible American invasion of that island, the Soviet Union might agree to withdraw them provided the American government publicly declared that it would never invade Cuba. Somewhat similar proposals were made by Valerian Zorin at the United Nations. It seemed that a solution had been found to the tightening crisis. Outside the White House, more than one thousand pickets marched carrying signs pleading for peace.

October 27: Yet another letter from Khrushchev dashed American hopes. It specified that American missiles stationed in Turkey must also be removed. Furthermore, at the United Nations, Soviet Ambassador Zorin was stating that American as well as Russian bases should undergo United Nations inspection. But much worse news was at hand.

A new Soviet ship capable of carrying missiles was found to be approaching Cuba with no apparent intention of stopping. Late reconnaissance photos showed continued feverish work on the Russian missile sites in Cuba. Two of the low-flying reconnaissance aircraft had drawn ground fire, and, worst of all, an American U-2 high-flying reconnaissance plane had been shot down by a Soviet ground-to-air missile.

The President's Council had prepared an automatic response to the shooting down of an American plane over Cuba. It consisted of a revenge air strike against a single ground-to-air missile site. This would be followed by an air strike against all such sites. It was expected that such a strike would bring forth Cuban MIG's and develop into an all-out battle for control of the air over Cuba. Russian technicians were bound to be killed in the fighting and bombing. But instead of allowing this plan to go automatically into effect, Kennedy decided to wait one more day. He authorized fighter escort for U.S. reconnaissance planes and warned American officials around the world, from besieged Berlin to strife-torn Laos, to prepare for the worst.

Meanwhile, the President's advisors prepared a letter to Khrushchev. In it they simply ignored the Soviet Premier's latest demands and concentrated instead on the reasonable proposals he had made in his letter of October 26. If the Soviet Union would undertake to stop all work on the Cuban missile sites and, under United Nations inspection and supervision, either remove or render inoperable those missiles presently stationed there, then the United States would be prepared to declare that it had no intention of invading Cuba to alter the government of Fidel Castro. In the interest of speed, this letter was issued publicly. But a private copy of it was delivered to the Russian ambassador in Washington by Attorney General Robert Kennedy with a verbal warning. The point of escalation was at hand. Unless the Soviet Union made up its mind immediately to accept the American terms, the United States was prepared to take "strong and overwhelming retaliatory action. . . ." In former times this verbal message would have been called an ultimatum. The "peril point" of the entire crisis was at hand.

October 28: Another letter from Khrushchev, transmitted publicly by Moscow stated that the Russians were prepared to accept the American terms. The missiles would be withdrawn and their sites dismantled

15

under United Nations supervision. The one Soviet ship still bound for Cuba had turned around to head for home. The Cuban missile crisis was over—as suddenly and dramatically as it had begun.

And the people of the world—especially the people of the United States—took a deep breath as they relaxed for the first time in a week. Mankind had been brought to the edge of an abyss; the civilization of the world had tottered momentarily on the lip of its own grave. Mingled with profound feelings of relief came the urgent questions. How had it all happened? How had it come to pass that the mighty super-powers were prepared to exterminate each other and probably most of the rest of the world over a small Caribbean island with a scanty population, few natural resources and no real strategic value (as had just been demonstrated to the Soviet Union's discomfiture)? The immediate answer—the establishment of Russian missile sites on Cuban soil—only raised other questions. How was it that an independent country of the Western Hemisphere had invited these missile sites? How was it that an island that had been little more than an American protectorate a few years before was now a Russian outpost? How was it that the Cuban revolution, which had seemingly eliminated an irresponsible "strong-man" government with all its vices in 1959, had apparently replaced it by 1962 with a government just as irresponsible and also dominated by a "strong man"?

The debate which had raged in the United States since 1959 over the merits or faults of the Cuban revolution and its leader, Fidel Castro, now took on graver meaning. Americans had taken a deeply emotional interest in the colorful escapades of the Cuban revolutionaries; they had felt a sense of personal rage and betrayal when it developed that the Cuban revolution was turning into a Communist takeover. Now, on the heels of the missile crisis, they realized that events on that tiny, languid tropical island could have the deepest international importance. And for many Americans, the most shocking discovery of all was that they simply *did not know* enough about Cuba, Cubans or the Cuban revolution itself to understand what had happened or why. Some Americans even took the bold step of actually cracking open their history books to find out what they could about Cuba. . . .

1

The Ever-Faithful Isle

The first mistake anyone ever made about Cuba was made by Christopher Columbus. The Admiral of the Ocean Sea discovered the island on October 28, 1492, during his first voyage of exploration. To his crew, the bright green coast rising out of the royal blue Caribbean looked like paradise—but to Columbus it looked like the mainland of Asia and so (in spite of the protests of some of his followers) he proclaimed it. He had already discovered Hispaniola to be an island, and he was determined to report the discovery of the mainland to his patrons, Ferdinand and Isabella, monarchs of Spain. Yet the Admiral's mistake was not based exclusively on wishful thinking (he resisted the temptation of sailing around the place to prove himself wrong), but also on appearances. For Cuba is more than 760 miles long and averages about 60 miles in width—a formidable land mass of almost 44,000 square miles (about the size of the state of Pennsylvania), with rugged mountain ranges visible from the sea—a place anyone might mistake for the mainland.

Later voyages of discovery corrected Columbus' first impression and also demonstrated that this huge island, because of its location, was the essential key to the exploration of much of the New World— and to its defense. Cuba is separated from the Florida Keys by the narrow Florida Strait, from Mexico by the Yucatan Channel, from Haiti by the Windward Passage—all of which are not so much barriers as they are narrow avenues of trade and warfare, easily controlled from Cuba. During the long age of sea power which Columbus' voyages inaugurated and which closed with the Second World War, possession of Cuba was the key to domination of the Caribbean Sea, the Gulf of Mexico and all the islands and coasts thereof—a fact commemorated by the key prominently displayed on the Cuban coat of arms.

Columbus took possession of Cuba (the name derives from the Indian word for the island, Cubanacán) for Spain, but it was not until 1511 that the first permanent Spanish settlement was established (at Baracoa on the north shore of what is now Oriente Province) under the guidance of Diego Velázquez, the island's first governor. The Spaniards brought horses, dogs, cattle and grain and during the next ten years founded the towns of Bayamo, Sancto Spiritus, Santiago de Cuba and San Cristóbal de la Havana (today's Havana, established on its present site in 1519). Under Spanish colonial policy, the land was parceled out to the settlers in vast *encomiendas*—plantations which were to be worked by local labor.

But the Spanish settlers soon found that the "local labor," which meant the native Indians of Cuba, was unsuited to heavy work—or to work of any kind. The Indians were peaceful, innocent (they were always described as "childlike"), and used to playing in the sun, gathering nuts and berries for their diet. The Spaniards easily enslaved them, but could not profit from that fact since once enslaved, the Indians had a disconcerting habit of simply sitting down and dying. Under the leadership of a local chieftain named Hatuey, the Indians did make one rebellion in 1514—only to be massacred by their masters. Appalled by his countrymen's treatment of the Indians (and well aware that such treatment was exactly contrary to official Spanish policy), a Dominican friar, Bartolome de Las Casas, hastened back to Spain in 1515 to plead the cause of the natives before the Spanish court. Although the good friar's protests soon resulted in a flood of edicts and proclamations from Madrid designed to protect the Indians (and earned Las Casas the title Apostle to the Indies), his efforts were too late to save the hapless natives of Cuba. Within a few decades they had been exterminated by harsh treatment, murder and disease. Beginning in 1523 they were increasingly replaced by Negro slaves imported from Africa.

Although Velázquez was a passably good administrator, the colony did not prosper. Men and materials were constantly being drained from Cuba to supply the various Spanish expeditions that conquered Mexico, Peru and Central America and for the explorations of such adventurers as Hernando de Soto, whose ill-starred expedition to Florida and the Mississippi started from Cuba. Furthermore, there was but little gold and silver in Cuba, and the attention of the Spanish government at home was riveted upon the more lucrative mines of the mainland.

But the capture and sack of Havana in 1555 by a French buccaneer, one Jacques de Sores, aroused the Council of the Indies in Madrid to the potential military and commercial value of the island. Havana was made an obligatory port of call for the richly laden Spanish treasure fleets plying from America to Spain—and was heavily fortified. Behind the guns of Morro Castle, the sixteenth-century citizens of Havana successfully beat off innumerable raids attempted against their city by French, Dutch and English privateers. Other Cuban towns not so heavily fortified were time and again ravaged by pirates.

The anarchy that reigned throughout the Caribbean during the seventeenth century, fueled by constant and complicated wars in Europe, retarded Cuba's growth. Few immigrants arrived, except for the three thousand Spanish colonists who were expelled from Jamaica when that island was captured by the British in 1655. Cubans had turned from the search for gold and silver to agriculture and the raising of cattle. Sugarcane had been planted, but it was cultivated only on a small scale. It was not until 1697, when the European powers settled their differences (temporarily at least) by the Treaty of Ryswick, that the threat of raids and war was lifted from Cuba.

A period of relative prosperity now set in, based primarily on Havana's prominence as a port and on the cultivation of tobacco. Shipbuilding in Havana doubled within fifty years of the Peace of Ryswick, while its trade (legally with the mother country, illegally with other American colonies) skyrocketed. So valuable did Cuba's tobacco crop become that it was made a monopoly of the Spanish government. But the rigid controls exercised from Madrid inflamed Cuba's *guajiros* (small landowners then) and resulted in several open revolts before the monopoly was ended in the eighteenth century. So important did Cuba now appear to Europeans that when Britain and Spain again found themselves at war (the Seven Years' War), a huge British force was dispatched to conquer the island. A British fleet appeared off Havana in June 1762 and, after a two-months' siege marked by heroism on both sides, captured the city. But the British occupation lasted only a year, ending with the Peace of Paris in 1763.

Again under Spanish authority, Havana's defenses were heavily strengthened, until it became the most strongly fortified city in the Western Hemisphere. Its strategic importance was underlined during the American Revolution. As an ally of France (which in turn was allied with the rebellious American colonies) Spain went again to war with England in 1779. Havana immediately became a very important base of operations. Expeditions went forth from this city to capture Mobile, Pensacola and the Bahamas from England—and French Admiral Comte François de Grasse set forth with his fleet to cut off General Cornwallis' troops at Yorktown, thus winning the final victory that assured American independence.

By that time Havana had become far and away the largest and in many respects the most beautiful city in the New World. Its population in 1774 was 76,000—more than twice that of New York, for example. It boasted parks, stately churches and palaces and an enlightened municipal government at a time when many North American cities were but glorified crossroads. And some of Havana's prosperity filtered out into the Cuban countryside—especially after 1791, when a new process for crystallizing sugar combined with a Spanish edict permitting free trade in slaves to give the Cuban sugar industry its real start toward the capture of world markets (and the saddling of Cuban agriculture with a "one-crop" economy).

By 1800 many of the ingredients that would combine to produce a century of rebellion, civil war and chaos on the island were already apparent in its social and economic life. One of these (which could be traced back to the days of Las Casas) was the independent attitude of the Spanish *grandees* of Cuba toward their home government. The descendants of the wealthier and more powerful of the original Spanish settlers owned vast plantations on which thousands of Negro slaves and propertyless white peasants labored under appalling conditions of poverty. Partly from sincere humanitarian concern, but primarily from a desire to exploit the wealth of Cuba for the benefit of the mother country, Spanish kings and governments had long rained decrees down upon the heads of the *colons,* the rich and (often) aristocratic lords of the island. But like *colons* before and since, the Spanish ruling class in Cuba was determined to exploit the wealth of their country for itself, not for a faraway government which increasingly lacked the means of asserting its authority. When threatened by foreign intervention or local rebellion, the Spanish *colons* looked to Spain for protection—but protection of their own personal local interests, not protection of Spanish sovereignty. When at times it appeared that *colon* exploitation of the island could best be served by alliance with foreign powers (especially the United States), the *colons* did not hesitate to betray Spain.

Another slow fuse burning through Cuban history was the condition to which most of the rest of the population had been reduced. The Indians had of course been wiped out (but not before a very few of them had mixed in or out of marriage with some of the Spanish settlers); Negroes remained slaves (except for a handful who had bought or been given their freedom from enlightened masters). Neither of these groups, then, though the most oppressed, was in any position to protest.

But there was yet another class of Cubans, and they formed the vast majority of whites on the island. These were the *guajiros,* descendants of those Spanish settlers who had received only small plots of land on their arrival in the New World. Originally the *guajiros*

21

were small independent farmers, raising food crops and tobacco mainly. But as Cuba's commerce prospered, first through tobacco and then through sugar, the *guajiros* found they could no longer compete with the vast plantations worked by slave labor. Their lands had been bought away from them, or they had been placed so deeply in debt that although they retained title to the land it was actually controlled by commercial interests in Havana.

By 1800 most *guajiros* had been reduced to either farm laborers or sharecroppers. But because sugarcane cultivation is a very seasonal operation, those who were farm laborers worked only a few months out of the year and at near starvation wages. Those who were share-croppers were trapped in the same round of indebtedness which was to make that system so vicious a feature of agricultural life in the South of the United States a few decades later. Seeds, tools, food and housing were supplied—at exorbitant prices—by the *patron* who owned the land. Labor was supplied by the *guajiro* and his family— for a share of the price the crop would bring when sold to wholesalers in Havana. Somehow the *guajiro's* share was never enough to pay off his yearly indebtedness to the *patron*. Even if it had been, the *guajiro* was illiterate and could never hope to figure out the complicated book-keeping of it all. *Guajiros* were as effectively enslaved as Negroes, but without the guarantee of food and shelter which slave owners pro-vided for their slaves.

Yet when Spain's South American colonies began winning their independence one after another in 1810, Cuba remained loyal to the mother country. There were several reasons. First of all, Cuba was cut off from the mainland, and hence to a certain extent was immune to the revolutionary agitation carried on by such leaders as Simón Bolívar. Not only was the island cut off, it quickly became a staging base for Spanish fleets and armies sent over to quell mainland re-bellions, so that the Spanish military presence on the island was far out of proportion to its population. Secondly, Cuban tobacco and sugar had enjoyed high prices and a large market during the Napo-leonic Wars, bringing great prosperity both to Spanish *grandees* and to the middle-class merchants of Havana. Some of this prosperity even trickled down to the *guajiros*. And, largely because they could not enforce restrictive commercial laws anyway, Spanish governments had adopted very liberal attitudes toward Cuban trade; that is, they did not seriously interfere with *colon* exploitation of Cuban natural wealth but were content to receive only those taxes which could realistically be collected. Thirdly, the white colonists, whether *grandees,* merchants or *guajiros,* with the recent terrible example of Toussaint L'Ouverture's successful Negro slave revolt in Haiti still vivid in their memory, feared to ignite any kind of revolutionary spark which might lead to a similar slave revolt in Cuba. And, finally, Cuba quickly became the refuge for all those Spanish officials and rich *colons* who were being driven out of South and Central America by revolutionary forces, and these were, of course, sworn and bitter enemies of independence. So Cuba watched while the rest of Spanish America won its freedom—and earned the title of the Ever-Faithful Isle from Spanish governments.

But the ideas set loose by the American and French Revolutions were not without some advocates in *La Isla Siempre Fidel.* In 1822 a young poet named José María de Heredia formed a secret society (romantically designed along Masonic lines, with secret handclasps, signs and rituals) whose aims were eventual independence from Spain and greater liberty at home. Although Heredia's group was discovered by the authorities and he himself was forced to flee into exile, his writings continued to inspire a new generation of Cubans.

Partly because of the uncovering of Heredia's plans, but mainly because of a change of government in Madrid (a short-lived constitutional government was replaced by new monarchical tyranny), beginning in 1823 Cuban liberties as well as the small amount of autonomy the island had previously enjoyed were wiped out. Spanish governors-general were granted absolute dictatorial powers over Cuba; freedom of the press was abolished in 1824; political prisoners began to crowd Havana's jails, and despotism settled like a permanent fog over the island.

The new repression was not long in claiming victims. In March 1826, Francisco de Agüero, a youth belonging to a well-known Camagüeyan family, was executed for revolutionary activities, thus becoming the first of a long line of Cuban martyrs to the struggle for

23

independence. Undismayed by Agüero's fate, two of his followers made their way to Colombia to interview the great South American revolutionary Simón Bolívar. Bolívar was prepared to lead an expedition to Cuba to win its independence, but the plan was never carried out, partly because of difficulties Bolívar faced at home and partly (as we shall see in the next chapter) because the plan was opposed by the United States. But new conspiracies kept bubbling up in Cuba: in 1837 and in 1844 colonial authorities uncovered plots against the government and promptly executed hundreds, including the very popular poet Gabriel Valdés, while forcing other hundreds to flee for their lives.

These early Cuban revolutionaries were basically well-educated, idealistic young men, of good family, but of widely varying backgrounds, and their aims were at best cloudy. Agüero, for example, was primarily interested in bringing an end to Spanish rule in Cuba. But while this was the aim of Valdés also, he demanded in addition the end of slavery in the island. There seemed to be general agreement that once the Spaniards were driven out, a Cuban government modeled after that of the United States would be set up. But the government of the United States meant different things to different Cubans. To the young idealists, especially those drawn from Havana's merchant class, it meant constitutional guarantees of liberty and representation in government. But to the wealthy landowning *colons* it meant a secure defense of the institution of slavery. If young idealists looked to the Declaration of Independence, the Constitution and other such justifications of popular government, the Cuban landowners looked to life in the nearby southern United States and to the increasingly ferocious defense of their own "peculiar institution" among American plantation owners against awakening American abolitionism. The landowning *colons* of Cuba were fearful that the Spanish government in Madrid might prove too weak to maintain slavery in Cuba. England had long since abolished slavery, and the British fleet was attempting to stamp out the slave trade throughout the world. It was possible that a Madrid government, bowing to British pressure or to the pressure of the increasingly vocal Roman Catholic opposition to Cuban slavery at home, might one day issue

24

the dreaded emancipation decree. But the United States was apparently a permanent and secure bastion of Negro bondage. So during the early decades of the nineteenth century, landowning *colons* in Cuba found themselves in strange alliance with young firebreathing idealists in agitating for independence.

The movement for Cuban independence was handicapped by the opposition of the Cuban merchant class and by the apathy and ignorance of the *guajiros*. Havana's merchants had interests diametrically opposed to those of the landowners. Regarding the issue of Negro slavery, they were basically indifferent. But their control of the sugar refineries and tobacco-curing plants as well as of the exportation of these enormously profitable staples was guaranteed (and not excessively taxed) by the Spanish government. A free Cuba, if it did not fall outright prey to the United States, would certainly be overwhelmed by a flood of Yankee dollars and businessmen who would wrest control from them of Cuba's commerce. During this period it was the merchants of Havana who were most vociferous in demanding harsher and harsher repressive measures from Spanish governors-general. As for the *guajiros,* they were sunk so deeply in poverty, illiteracy and despair that even if they had ever been called upon to strike a blow for independence they could not have responded.

The dismantling of slavery in the United States following the American Civil War completely changed the complexion of revolutionary movements in Cuba. For the most part, Cuban landowners now saw that their only remaining hope for maintaining slavery in Cuba lay with the government in Madrid, and they thereupon once again switched their allegiance and became the most fanatical of supporters of continued Spanish rule. On the other hand, some of the more enlightened landowning *colons* suddenly realized not only that slavery was most probably doomed in any event in Cuba, but that it was economically unsound. The pre-Civil War experience of the Southern Confederacy and the great industrial advances of the North just before and during the Civil War were not lost upon them. They realized that greater profits might be had by combining industrialization with free labor. Furthermore, they were increasingly resentful of the stranglehold on their export and import trade exercised by the

25

Havana merchants under Spanish protection. Meanwhile, the good news from the north slowly filtered down into Cuba's slave pens and plantations. Negro slaves on the island realized that freedom could be won after all, and began to join secret revolutionary movements and conspiracies. Even the *guajiros,* feeling the shock waves from the American Civil War, were coming to understand that their poverty and despair were not necessarily permanent decrees of heaven but the result of their exploitation by *colons* and merchants.

The most immediate result of all this ferment was the outbreak of the Ten Years' War in Cuba. On October 10, 1868, an enlightened landowner and lawyer of Oriente Province, Carlos Manuel de Céspedes, freed his slaves, gathered a band of Negroes, *guajiros* and young idealists around him and raised the standard of revolt at the village of Yara. In nearby Camagüey Province another landowner, Salvador Cisneros, with the help of a lawyer, Ignacio Agramonte, raised other revolutionary groups. The rebels proclaimed the independence of Cuba, drew up a constitution modeled on that of the United States, and in 1869 proclaimed Carlos Manuel de Céspedes "president" of their revolutionary "government."

The rebels won several victories in pitched battles against isolated Spanish garrisons at first. Agramonte revealed a great natural talent for war and organized a cavalry which was more than a match for the Spaniards. *Guajiros* and Negroes flocked to the rebel banners, while rebel emissaries in New York and Boston desperately tried to enlist American money and support for the revolution. Agramonte was killed in a Spanish ambush in 1873, but command of his cavalry fell into the hands of an equally brilliant military leader, Máximo Gómez. In 1874, Céspedes (who had earlier been forced to resign as "president" because of internal dissensions in the rebel camp) was captured by the Spaniards and shot. But shortly afterwards, Máximo Gómez with 1,300 infantry and 300 cavalry defeated a much larger Spanish regular army force at Las Guásimas, the Spaniards losing more than 400 killed. But this was to prove the last victory of the rebellion.

The *guajiros,* the Negroes and the young idealists who composed the backbone of the rebel forces during the Ten Years' War were ill-supplied and poorly trained. They fought bravely and endured untold hardships for years while hiding in the mountains, but they were no match in open battle for the well-equipped, heavily drilled reinforcements that Spain continued to pour into the island. The only rebel hope lay in maintaining a *guerrilla* ("little war") campaign against the Spanish army, with the essential help and support of the rural population. But as the war dragged on for years and years, the suffering among the peasants and slaves of Oriente and Camagüey Provinces reached epic proportions. Entire districts were depopulated; crops vanished from the fields; towns and hamlets were burned out: the necessary base for a successful guerrilla campaign was destroyed. Furthermore, though many Americans sympathized with the rebels, the United States government, far from aiding them either openly or surreptitiously, refused even to recognize their belligerent status.

A new Spanish commander in Cuba, General Arsenio Martínez de Campos, correctly gauging the situation, offered the rebels terms and reforms. On February 10, 1878, he signed, along with the remaining rebel leaders, the Convention of El Zanjón, which spoke vaguely of reform and granted Cuba an increased measure of autonomy from Spanish rule. A precarious peace followed, and of course the promised reforms were watered down again and again until they finally disappeared. Nevertheless, one reform did take place. Unable to further withstand pressure from other civilized countries, with the specter of slave revolt still fresh in memory from the thousands of Negroes who had supported the rebel cause during the Ten Years' War, and with the grudging acceptance of a landowning *colon* class that was at last prepared to substitute wage slavery for the real thing, the Spanish government abolished slavery in Cuba in 1886. Former Negro slaves were now free to join the long-suffering *guajiros* in absolute poverty.

The wobbly peace that followed the Ten Years' War was to be upset by one of the most romantic and perhaps the greatest leader ever to arise in Cuba, José Julián Martí. Born in 1853 in Havana of humble Spanish immigrant parents, Martí taught himself to read and write. Later he studied with a brilliant tutor. Martí was to become the greatest of Cuban writers and one of the greatest writers in the entire Spanish-speaking world. He was imprisoned in Havana in 1868 for

27

José Julián Martí

writing pamphlets in support of the rebels who had just launched the Ten Years' War (he was just sixteen at the time) and was exiled to Spain. He took advantage of his exile to study and travel, visiting France, the United States, several South American countries and, when it seemed safe, Cuba from time to time. Everywhere he went he spoke for Cuban independence, collected money to support Cuban rebel groups, tried to enlist support among Cuban emigrés from New York to Buenos Aires, and wrote articles and pamphlets calling for freedom. His one-man crusade abroad can be compared only to the tireless efforts of that other great nineteenth century revolutionary, China's Doctor Sun Yat-sen.

While living in New York, Martí gathered together some of the surviving military leaders of the Ten Years' War who also lived in exile and formed the Cuban Revolutionary Party in 1892. He raised funds, enlisted promises of support from various American adventurers, and launched small "kindling" expeditions against Cuba. One of these "kindling" expeditions finally set fire to Oriente Province on February 24, 1895, at the town of Baire, where the standard of open rebellion was again raised. Martí at once issued a manifesto to the Cuban people calling for complete independence and a republican form of government. Then, despite the protests of Cuban leaders who felt he was too valuable to the cause to take risks, Martí insisted on accompanying the doughty old warrior Máximo Gómez (the same veteran of the Ten Years' War) back to Cuba to lead the revolt personally. He was killed a few days later during a skirmish with Spanish troops, leaving his countrymen an imperishable legend and example.

The remaining leaders of the Revolution of 1895 as it came to be called, organized a revolutionary government on September 13, 1895, with Salvador Cisneros (the same landowner who had launched the Ten Years' War) as president. Meanwhile, Máximo Gómez and his principal lieutenant, Antonio Maceo, gathered recruits and began raiding Spanish outposts. They won notable victories at Peralejo (where they almost captured Spanish General Martínez de Campos) and at Mal Tiempo near Havana. So successful were the guerrilla tactics of Gómez and Maceo that they actually reached the outskirts of Havana itself in January 1896. But they could not hope to topple that heavily fortified bastion and so retired to the center of the island to continue their campaign. All Spanish efforts to trap Gómez and Maceo failed ignominiously.

But the Spanish government was determined to stamp out this latest rebellion on the Ever-Faithful Isle, and to that end dispatched more than 100,000 regular troops there. Perhaps of greater importance, the bumbling General Martínez de Campos was replaced by General Valeriano Weyler, a much sterner and more efficient soldier. Recognizing that the rebel guerrilla campaign depended on the rural population for support and concealment, Weyler determined to attack the very base of the rebellion by simply removing the rural population from vast areas of the countryside. Thousands and thousands of *guajiros* were rounded up and forced into "reconcentration camps" established by Weyler near Havana. There they subsisted on the charity of local or American food contributions and died like flies of malnutrition and disease. For those who were lucky enough to escape the reconcentration camps, life under Weyler was not much better. He embarked on an organized campaign of terrorism in the country-side and the burning-out of fields and towns where rebels might hide or from which they might draw sustenance. The rebels retaliated by burning sugar plantations throughout the island. Within a year Cuba had sunk into anarchy and starvation.

Nonetheless, Weyler's policies were winning. Maceo was caught in ambush and killed in Havana Province in December 1896; rebel forces were being forced back up into the mountains and rebel policies of responding to Weyler's terrorism with terrorism of their own were eating into *guajiro* support for the revolutionary cause. But just as Weyler's repression began to produce results, a new Spanish government more liberal than its predecessor came into power in Madrid. Bowing to United States protests, the Liberals recalled General Weyler and replaced him by the milder General Ramón Blanco, who was named governor-general in September 1897. He was empowered to offer the Cubans almost complete autonomy in their home government. Unfortunately, this offer which might have been accepted three years before was now too late. The Cuban rebels, sensing the imminence of American intervention, would accept nothing less than total independence. On the other hand, the merchants of Havana and many of the landowning *colons* would tolerate no concessions at all to the revolutionists. When General Blanco arrived in Havana he was greeted with carefully staged riots promoted by the Havana merchants through their reactionary club, the Casino Español. The rioters enjoyed the tacit and sometimes active support of Spanish army and navy officers who feared that any settlement with the rebels would tarnish their honor.

Now it so happened that the American consul-general in Havana at that time was Fitzhugh Lee, a former Confederate cavalry commander and a man of small diplomatic gifts but with a choleric temper. Worried that the anti-Blanco riots might spread and be directed against American business enterprises and individuals in Cuba (the *colons*

30

were well aware that the American government was exerting pressure on Spain to grant Cuba autonomy or independence), Fitzhugh Lee demanded protection. The protection arrived immediately in the form of the powerful U.S. battleship *Maine,* which appeared in Havana harbor in January 1898. And although no anti-American riots took place, the big ship remained there until the night of February 15, 1898. On that night all of Havana was rocked by a tremendous explosion that seemed to have occurred in the harbor. . . .

2

The Yankee Meddler

American interest in Cuban affairs went back to the early days of the Republic and was itself the other continuing thread in the tangled skein of Cuban political life. As early as 1823, in a strangely inconsistent burst of imperial fever, Thomas Jefferson suggested that the island be annexed to the United States. But when, at the call of Simón Bolívar, a "Panama Congress" of Latin American patriots met in 1825 (the same Congress to which Agüero's followers went in 1826) to organize various *pronunciamentos,* conspiracies and plots to bring about a Cuban revolution, the American representatives at the Congress were instructed to avoid any involvement whatsoever in its deliberations. These representatives had been sent by the administration of John Quincy Adams, who saw clearly enough that if Cuba won her independence she would not be able to maintain it: sooner or later she would fall into the power of another and stronger European state, perhaps France, probably England. This would pose a threat to the United States far greater than any posed by the vitiated and lethargic ambitions of Spain.

Real or imaginary designs on Cuba had already been countered by President James Monroe when he enunciated his celebrated Doctrine. And for twenty years following the Panama Congress, American policy continued to support Spanish rule in Cuba.

Just as Cuban loyalties (at least on the part of the landowning *colons*) were conditioned by the existence of slavery and, as they saw it, the necessity for its preservation, so American attitudes toward Cuba were influenced by the existence of slavery in the United States. In the years preceding our own Civil War, Southern statesmen such as Clay and Calhoun saw in the annexation of Cuba a vital extension of slavery against the expanding power of the North—while to the more belligerent and light-minded sons of the Southern aristocracy, seizure of the island seemed to promise adventure and plunder.

Besides this overriding economic motive, in America there was Manifest Destiny—that curious and semidivine philosophical justification for conquest that afflicted Americans, north as well as south, in recurrent cycles all during the nineteenth century. By the 1850s Americans had already explained Manifest Destiny to the irritated British in the Oregon Territories and with greater success had inflicted it upon the hapless Mexicans at Vera Cruz and Chapultepec. To many Americans it seemed only "manifest" that Cuba should be next on their menu. And of course there was always a strain of sincere proselytization in American motives. To the enlightened inheritors of the Puritan ideal in flowering New England, a crusade to liberate Cuba from the twin evils of Spanish tyranny and Papist influence seemed at times a moral obligation. It was this combination of interests—sometimes articulate, mostly obscurely understood—which led to a continuing series of American attempts upon the island.

The most notable of these attempts was that led by General Narcisco Lopez in 1851. Lopez, although a Venezuelan, had been a general in the Spanish army, a senator in the Spanish Cortes (Parliament) and governor of Madrid. His loyalty had been rewarded by a post in Cuba, where at the behest of some of the landowning *colons* (then in their period of longing for American protection for slavery) he organized an uprising. When his conspiracy failed he fled the island with a Spanish price on his head, to attempt raising a liberating army in the United States. Lopez established himself in New Orleans, where he found funds, arms, and ardent local support. He assured his American backers that the Cuban people were only awaiting his arrival on Cuban soil to rally around his banner and throw off the Spanish yoke. That banner, incidentally, with its five bars and single star, which was to become the flag of the Cuban Republic, was, appropriately, first flown from a staff atop the offices of the *New York Sun* in 1850.

In August 1851, at the head of an "army" of about five hundred mercenaries—mostly American, German and Polish soldiers of fortune, with four dozen Cubans mixed in for appearances—General Lopez set sail on his crusade. The expedition landed at Playtas, about sixty miles west of Havana, on August 11. Unfortunately, the Cuban people failed to rally around this international brigade, and within ten days the adventurers had been rounded up by the Spanish army. A few of the survivors were executed at Havana—General Lopez himself being garroted for high treason—while the rest were packed off to the Spanish penal colonies in Africa. The Americans who a century later planned the Bay of Pigs disaster were evidently unfamiliar with the melancholy story of General Lopez.

But Lopez' failure did not dampen American, especially Southern, interest in Cuba. In 1854 the American ministers to France, England and Spain (all pro-slavery men), while gathered to take the waters at the fashionable spa at Ostend, Belgium, issued a highly original manifesto in which they urged the State Department to offer Spain $120,000,000 for Cuba, and in the event that Spain refused to sell, to seize the island by force. While the Ostend Manifesto may have astonished the foreign ministries of the world, it only alerted the North to what was now becoming very clear: Southern interest in Cuba threatened an extension of the slave power. In the face of adamant abolitionist opposition, further attempts against the Ever-Faithful Isle came to nothing. Then the storm of Civil War absorbed American passions, and when it was over, the abolition of slavery had ended the original economic basis of our interest in Cuban affairs.

Americans were not to become excited again over Cuba until 1873, when the celebrated *Virginius* affair pricked the national temper. The *Virginius,* flying the American flag, was a vessel which, under the command of various freebooters, had for years been running guns to various revolutionary groups in Central America and the Caribbean. When the Ten Years' War broke out in Cuba in 1868, the *Virginius* added the Cuban insurrectionaries to her list of customers. But in October 1873 her luck ran out. She was caught on the high seas by a Spanish gunboat and brought into the port of Santiago de Cuba. Her cargo was discovered to consist of rifles and ammunition while her "passengers" were evidently Cuban revolutionaries.

Under international law, a ship of neutral registry cannot be apprehended on the high seas outside territorial waters, no matter what her cargo or mission, especially when no state of war exists. Furthermore, as American citizens, some of the crew of the *Virginius* enjoyed special protection from overzealous local authorities under a Spanish-American treaty dating back to 1795. But to the *colon* mentality Madrid was as distant as Washington, and gunrunners like the *Virginius* were seldom caught. The local Spanish authorities, urged on by the *colons,* decided to make of the ship and her crew an example. Accordingly both the crew and the passengers of the *Virginius* were tried before a drumhead military court-martial aboard a Spanish gunboat in Santiago Bay. On November 1, 1873, the court sentenced all of them to death. With great dispatch local officials proceeded immediately to execute their prisoners in batches—Cubans, Americans and some British found aboard. They had succeeded in killing fifty-three of them before consular protests, frantic cables from Madrid and, most effective of all, the arrival of a British man-of-war cleared for action in Santiago harbor put an end to the slaughter.

The war cry was immediately raised in the United States and the Navy was mobilized at Key West. But Secretary of State Hamilton Fish succeeded, after prolonged negotiations, in extracting apologies and an indemnity from Madrid, while in the United States it soon became clear that not only was the *Virginius* a gunrunner and her crew filibusterers, but she was owned by Cuban insurrectionists and was probably not entitled to fly the American flag anyhow. Furthermore, it was suddenly realized that the United States had allowed its Navy to sink to such a level of decrepitude that the collection of antique hulks at Key West would probably have lost a battle to any

36

maritime power in the world—even Spain. So the war fever died out. But it lead President Ulysses S. Grant to some interesting reflections upon the Cuban revolutionary movement. "During the whole contest," he wrote, "the ramshackle exhibition has been made of large numbers of Cubans escaping from the island and avoiding the risks of war, congregating in this country at a safe distance from the scene of danger, and endeavoring to make war from our shores, to urge our people into the fight, which they avoid, to embroil this government in complications and possible hostilities with Spain. It can scarce be doubted that this last result is the real object of these parties. . . ."

Although President Grant's statement was unfair to the Cuban revolutionaries who were fighting heroically and suffering great hardship during the Ten Years' War at home, he was undoubtedly correct about many of the Cuban exiles. His words, evidently forgotten by succeeding generations of Americans, sound a prophetic knell in contemporary ears.

With the end of the Ten Years' War in 1879 and the abolition of slavery in Cuba in 1886, American investment in island industry began to grow at a rapid pace. The Madrid government, unable, because of chaotic political conditions and economic depression at home, to supply the necessary capital for the expansion of Cuban sugar production to meet a growing North American and world demand (by 1890 fully 90% of all sugar consumed in the United States came from Cuba), permitted and even encouraged foreign investment. American dollars began to flow into Cuba, and American refinery managers and plantation overseers followed the dollars. By 1898 the Cuban sugar industry would be more than 50% controlled by American interests. But while Cuban sugar exports expanded with this stimulus of Yankee money, the Cuban economy became more and more dependent on the United States as the prime purchaser of Cuba's prime product. In 1893 the Cuban economy suffered a heavy blow as part of the worldwide depression of that year. But this blow was turned into a disaster the following year by the American Tariff Bill of 1894 which imposed high import duties on Cuban sugar. It was this economic collapse which prepared the ground for José Julián Martí's Revolution of 1895.

Martí's endless agitation among Cuban emigrés had been eminently successful in the United States. The Cuban "colonies" of New York, New Orleans and Florida were organized into two hundred clubs affiliated under the title of the Cuban Revolutionary Party. Each member was required to devote one-tenth of his personal income to the cause of Cuban independence, and by 1895 it was estimated that over one million dollars had been collected. It was this money that financed the return of Máximo Gómez and Martí to Cuba in February of that year. In the long run, perhaps of greater importance was the fact that some of these heavily involved Cuban exiles were American citizens and almost all of them had American relatives or friends.

But aside from the connections of Cuban exiles and the heavy investment of American money in Cuba's sugar industry, there were other, perhaps weightier reasons for increased American attention to the island during the last years of the nineteenth century. In the decades following the Civil War, the United States had become one of the greatest industrial nations on earth—as it was only now beginning to realize. Giant new American industries required foreign markets, and foreign markets required both a large Navy to protect American commerce and bases from which that Navy could operate in the days when ships steamed on coal within a limited radius. The writings of American Naval Captain Alfred T. Mahan were focusing not only American but world attention for the first time on the true importance and nature of sea power in history. If American commerce in Asia was to flourish, the United States required bases in the Far East; if a canal was to be dug across Panama or Nicaragua, the United States required Caribbean bases to protect it. In the minds of such imperialists as Mahan and the young Theodore Roosevelt, it was already clear that a war with Spain would provide both. From Spain the Philippine Islands might be seized in the Far East and Cuba in the Caribbean. Although the economic basis of imperialist fever was at best theoretical for the United States (American businessmen almost unanimously opposed war with Spain or anyone else as economically risky), this did not seem to deter American jingos from wanting to flex the national muscle.

38

The industrialization that had given an impulse to American imperialism had also brought with it terrible domestic problems. American labor was the unwelcome guest at the national table— grossly underpaid, unorganized, put down by the courts, savaged by hired regiments of thugs when it attempted to strike, massacred by federal and National Guard troops when it fought back. Only slightly better off were American farmers whose lands were being gobbled up by giant corporations, who had to pay unfair railroad freight rates, and who were caught in a scarcity-of-money squeeze by eastern banks and mortgage companies. All of these and others rallied in 1896 behind the banners of the Democratic candidate for the presidency, William Jennings Bryan, in one of the most bitterly fought election campaigns in American history. Some Republican supporters of William McKinley thought they saw in the imperial fever an excellent means of diverting public attention from domestic wrongs, and they used it ruthlessly.

Thus Republican members of the United States Senate, seeking to make as much trouble as possible for the outgoing Democratic administration of President Grover Cleveland, in 1896 forced through a resolution "that the independence of the Republic of Cuba be and the same is hereby acknowledged by the United States of America." This interesting attempt by the Senate to take over the President's constitutional prerogatives in foreign affairs was rejected by Cleveland's Secretary of State, Richard Olney, who stated: "The resolution will be without effect and will leave unaltered the attitude of this government toward the two contending parties in Cuba." But the incoming President, William McKinley, was by no means so courageous or honest as his predecessor and could offer but little resistance to imperialist pressures.

Finally, of surprisingly great importance in the web of events that led to war was the emergence of "yellow journalism" in the United States, especially as exemplified by the newspaper "war" then being waged in New York by Joseph Pulitzer's *World* and William Randolph Hearst's *Journal*. These two newspapers, striving for ever greater circulation, seemed determined to see which of them could appeal to the basest tastes of the most readers. In their struggle, imperialism and war fever were potent weapons. They did not hesitate to falsify or even to create news to sell papers.

An example of the ferocity of this newspaper contest was the report by correspondent Richard Harding Davis of February 12, 1897, to the *Journal* that the United States mail steamer *Olivette* had been boarded in Havana harbor by Spanish police officials who thereupon seized, stripped and searched three young Cuban ladies. Under a huge headline demanding "DOES OUR FLAG PROTECT WO-MEN?" the *Journal* offered its readers a vivid drawing by Frederick Remington showing three sinisterly bearded Spaniards leering at a naked young girl. But before American outrage could express itself officially, Mr. Pulitzer's energetic young men on the *World* proved the Davis story a fraud. They called on one of the young ladies in-volved and were informed that the search had been conducted by a police matron in the privacy of a cabin. But Mr. Hearst only shrugged and prepared for the next bogus scandal. Newspaper readers who (without radio or television) depended entirely on the press for in-formation from the outside world were successfully whipped into anger and even hysteria by such false reporting. When in later years William Randolph Hearst was to claim the Spanish-American War as "his own," he exaggerated only slightly.

Dimly aware of the forces pushing the United States into open intervention in Cuba, President McKinley spent months negotiating with Madrid, urging the Spanish government to grant Cuba greater autonomy if not outright independence. It was through American promptings that General Weyler (who had been labeled "Butcher Weyler" in the American press) was withdrawn and General Ramón Blanco sent to make his fruitless offers to the Cuban rebels. But the truth was that no Spanish government could grant independence to Cuba without risking revolution at home, so shaky was the political base of the Spanish monarchy. Making concession after concession to American demands, well aware that they would certainly lose any war with the United States but equally determined not to give up Spain's first and last American possession without a fight, the Spanish government tried desperately to avoid the inevitable.

40

This then was the long background of American-Cuban-Spanish relations which focused down onto the visit of the U.S. battleship *Maine* to Havana; this was the long fuse which ignited when, on the night of February 15, 1898, that terrible explosion rocked Havana harbor. It was an explosion that sank the *Maine* and carried 258 of her crew to a watery grave—and made war between the United States and Spain over Cuba certain.

Who sank the *Maine*? The U.S. Naval Board of Inquiry, which was immediately convened to investigate, declared that the ship was sunk by an outside agency although it did not specify who might be responsible. Certainly neither the Spanish government nor its military and naval representatives in Havana were responsible. Not only were they trying desperately to *avoid* war with the United States, but such a wholesale assassination was utterly outside the Spanish character. Cuban rebels might have committed the crime precisely in the hope of embroiling Spain and the United States, but it was extremely unlikely that they had the means or the ability to do it, or that they would have been willing to risk the terrible consequences of discovery. On the other hand, the fire-eating *colons* of Havana who hated the United States and the Spanish government almost equally probably could have mustered the means. And recent experience of the *colon* mentality—as exhibited, for example, in Algeria during the 1950s— has demonstrated the savage lengths to which such people will go to maintain their privileged way of life in a subject country. But most probably, despite the Naval Board's findings, the *Maine* blew up from internal causes. The combination on a steel warship of electricity, coal gas, and improved gunpowder was not fully understood in those days: more than seventeen large warships belonging to various nations blew up from internal causes between 1889 and 1902.

None of this mattered to the American people, especially the readers of the yellow press. No matter who struck the spark, somehow Spain was to be held responsible. The war cry "Remember the *Maine*, to hell with Spain!" rang through the country and through the halls of Congress. Last-minute negotiations between McKinley and the Spanish government (in which Spain acceded to practically all the President's requests) could not dampen the war fever. On April 19, 1898 (it had taken the Naval Board of Inquiry several weeks to issue its report), the United States Congress passed a resolution calling for the forcible expulsion of Spain from Cuba. The vote was not unanimous—many Senators honorably opposed war. One of these, Senator Henry M. Teiler, managed to tack an amendment onto the resolution which stated:

That the United States hereby disclaims any disposition or intention to exercise sovereignty, jurisdiction or control over said island, except for the pacification thereof, and asserts its determination when that is accomplished to leave the government and control of the island to its people.

It was notable that at no time did the American Congress show any real intention of recognizing the revolutionary Cuban Republic (a resolution to that effect was tossed out) about which they had previously expressed so much concern. It was now suddenly discovered that the revolutionary movement founded by José Martí whose forces were still fighting the Spaniards under the leadership of Máximo Gómez did not, after all, represent enough of the Cuban people to deserve recognition. Only the Teller Amendment stood between Cuban independence and American annexation of the island. It was to prove an embarrassing but not insurmountable obstacle.

Nevertheless, while the *colons* of Havana fumed and the Cuban revolutionaries in the hills celebrated and the Spanish government shuddered, members of Congress gathered outside the Senate chamber to sing, "There'll Be a Hot Time in the Old Town Tonight!"—and Cuban and American histories, which had so often and so painfully touched each other over the years, fused at last.

The "splendid little war" (as John Hay called it) against Spain lasted, effectively, only three months. On May 1, 1898, Commodore George Dewey's Asiatic Squadron fell upon the collection of naval antiques that Spain called its Far Eastern Fleet in Manila Bay and dispatched them before breakfast—thereby assuring the United States of a large Far Eastern colony, a prolonged and bloody war against Filipino insurrectionists, all the headaches of "the White Man's Burden," and, eventually, war with Japan in the next century.

At first it was thought that the United States had only to arm and supply the Cuban revolutionaries, while blockading the island, to bring about the collapse of the Spanish power there. But it soon appeared that to do either would require, first, sinking the Spanish Atlantic fleet and, second, landing a large expeditionary force. The Spanish Atlantic Squadron of four cruisers and a handful of torpedo boats obligingly crossed the ocean (everyone aboard, from Admiral Pascual Cervera down to the midshipmen, knowing they were sailing to their doom) and was bottled up in the harbor of Santiago de Cuba by the vastly more powerful United States fleet. And on June 22 a miserably under-equipped, poorly led, and disorganized American Expeditionary Force landed at Daiquiri and Siboney with the help of Cuban *guerril-leros* (and the incredible inefficiency of the Spanish army). From there they launched an attack on Santiago to drive the Spanish squadron to sea.

Fighting was sharp at Las Guasimas and El Caney; Teddy Roose-velt led his Rough Riders in their famous charge (on foot!) up San Juan Hill, and eventually, on July 3, 1898, Admiral Cervera was forced to order his ships to make a run for it. Under Admiral William T. Sampson, the much larger American fleet guarding Santiago harbor promptly gave chase. As Captain Victor M. Concas y Palau of the Spanish cruiser *Maria Theresa* heard his bugler calling battle stations, he reflected: "The sound of my bugles was the last echo of those which history tells us were sounded at the capture of Granada. It was the signal that the history of four centuries of grandeur was at an end and that Spain was becoming a nation of the fourth class." Captain Concas was correct. Within a few hours all the Spanish ships had been sunk or run down, the last of them to limp to the shore being named after the man who had started the whole cycle of Cuban history ending that day—the *Cristobal Colon*.

On July 17 the Spaniards surrendered Santiago, and the following day the Spanish government put out peace feelers. Later that month an American expedition seized Puerto Rico (where no Teller Amend-ment prevented annexation), and on August 12 Spanish and American representatives signed an armistice. This was followed by a peace treaty signed in Paris on December 10, 1898, in which Spain ceded

43

the Philippines, Guam and other small mid-Pacific islands and Puerto Rico to the United States. When the Spaniards suggested that the United States annex Cuba to protect Spaniards living there from Cuban insurrectionist vengeance, the offer was haughtily turned aside as not consistent with the Teller Amendment. Instead a separate treaty was signed which provided for American military occupation of the island to "combat starvation and disease." The last Spanish troops withdrew from Cuba on January 1, 1899, as the United States Army took over. The retiring Spanish authorities derived what comfort they could from the grim reflection that from now on Cuba was going to be someone else's headache. The question was: Whose?

3

Dollar Diplomats and Dictators

The American view of how much Cuban participation would be allowed in Cuban affairs was indicated by the fact that Cuban representatives were excluded from the Paris Peace Conference that settled Cuba's fate. Sixty years later, Cuban students in an "open letter" to American students were to declare: "After our people had fought for over ninety years for their independence amid conspiracies, scaffolds, exiles and insurrections, this was their reward." During the war itself, although Cuban guerrilla forces provided much help for the American Expeditionary Force, they were not invited to witness the surrender of Santiago. Nor were they consulted when the United States appointed General Leonard Wood to be military governor of Cuba on December 13, 1899.

General Wood did well those things which American military governors generally do well: he inaugurated a highway construction program, introduced an efficient sanitation program (under his regime the scourge of yellow fever was largely lifted from the island) and reorganized the local school system. But he also did other things that American military governors generally do. He "reformed" the courts but kept the archaic Spanish legal code in effect, and he took particular care to protect American business investments in Cuba even when this meant extensive cooperation with those very land-owning and merchant ex-*colons* who had so bitterly opposed the Cuban revolution.

General Wood, on instructions from Washington, also supervised the election of delegates to a Cuban Constitutional Convention in September 1900. He instructed the delegates to include in their new constitution a provision "upon the relations to exist between that [the United States] government and the government of Cuba." The Convention dutifully met and wrote a constitution modeled after that of the United States. But the delegates refused to incorporate any humiliating clauses in the basic law of their land regarding their association with a foreign power.

If the Cubans would not define their relations with the United States, the U.S. Senate was prepared to do so whether they liked it or not. The result was the infamous Platt Amendment to a Congressional Army Appropriations Bill passed on March 2, 1901. The amendment declared that control of Cuba would be turned over to Cubans only after American interests had been secured. The revelant articles of the amendment read:

The Government of Cuba consents that the United States may exercise the right to intervene for the preservation of Cuban independence, the maintenance of a government adequate for the protection of life, property and individual liberty, and for discharging the obligations with respect to Cuba imposed by the Treaty of Paris on the United States, now to be assumed and undertaken by the Government of Cuba.

To enable the United States to maintain the independence of Cuba, and to protect the people thereof, as well as for its own defense, the Cuban Government will sell or lease to the United States the land necessary for coaling or naval stations, at certain specified points, to be agreed upon with the President of the United States.

The Cuban delegates at their Constitutional Convention objected bitterly to the Platt Amendment. They even went so far as to send a delegation to Washington to protest against it. The members of this delegation were met by Secretary of War Elihu Root and told: "This clause does not diminish Cuban independence; it leaves Cuba independent and sovereign under its own flag. The United States will only come to its rescue in extreme cases to help Cuba to preserve its absolute independence, and God grant this extremity never be presented. It (the clause) may even come to be forever unknown by the masses of Cubans, its existence being known only to students of political history. . . ."

As there was nothing they could do about it, the Cuban delegates obediently incorporated the Platt Amendment as an Appendix to the Cuban Constitution on June 12, 1901. It was as if the American Constitutional Convention meeting at Philadelphia in 1787 had adopted, as a permanent part of the United States Constitution, a clause permitting their former allies, the French (whose strength had done very much to win American independence), to intervene in American affairs whenever the French government decided it was necessary, and to maintain French naval and army stations on the eastern seaboard. And far from becoming "forever unknown by the masses of Cubans," the Platt Amedment was to become a running sore in Cuban-American relations and a hateful symbol of Yankee domination to those very masses.

Nevertheless, the bitter pill was swallowed; American Naval and Marine bases were established at Guantánamo Bay and Bahía Honda, and in December 1901 elections held under the new constitution for a Cuban government. Tómas Estrada Palma took office as Cuba's first president in 1902, and the first Cuban Congress convened early in May of that same year. General Leonard Wood formally surrendered his executive powers on May 20, 1902, to the new Cuban government, and that day (not, be it noted, the day *Spanish* rule ended) was ever afterward to be celebrated as Cuban Independence Day.

President Estrada Palma was an honest administrator but a weak and inadequate political leader. His party, the Moderates, was opposed by the Liberal Party, but the differences in outlook between these two political groupings were even less than those which divide Republicans and Democrats in the United States. Both parties supported a capital-

47

ist development of Cuban resources and favored large-scale foreign investment in the island to bring this about. Essentially, both parties represented the landowners and the merchants of Havana. Illiteracy and an apathy bred of centuries of oppression effectively eliminated the *guajiros,* white and black alike, from political influence and even from participation.

Because he lacked confidence in his popularity, when Palma stood for reelection in 1905 he permitted his followers to resort to fraud. The amazingly large figure of 150,000 false names were registered by the Moderate Party during the primary elections that year. Liberal Party leaders and voters, perceiving the fraud, declared that they would simply stay away from the polls on election day. They did, and Palma was reelected and inaugurated for his second term in the spring of 1906. Palma's opponent, Liberal Party leader José Miguel Gómez (no shining example of political virtue himself, but highly popular with Cubans), declared that Palma's fraudulent reelection was the "direct responsibility" of the United States government and that open rebellion against the Palma government was prevented only by Palma's repeated warnings that any revolt against his presidency would cause the United States to "immediately send troops to chastise" the rebels.

Nevertheless, open revolt did break out when Palma was inaugurated in 1906. By fall of that year more than 15,000 insurrectionist troops were gathered around Havana, and President Palma begged President Theodore Roosevelt to intervene. Roosevelt, a bit reluctantly, agreed. He sent Secretary of War William Howard Taft to Cuba and dispatched 24,000 American troops to back him up (United States Marines, summoned from Guantánamo by the nervous American chargé d'affaires at the Havana embassy, were already patrolling the streets of the capital). President Palma quickly retired, and Taft established himself as provisional governor of Cuba in 1906. He was soon replaced by Charles E. Magoon, about whose administration of Cuban affairs Cubans were later to write: "Estrada Palma, with all his political defects, which were great, was an honorable and austere administrator of public affairs. When Magoon and the North American provisional government came, our administrative methods became corrupt and perverted." While this charge may be exaggerated (Cuban politicians needed no outside lessons in corruption), it was certainly true that Magoon, as the head of this first massive American intervention in Cuban affairs, placed American interests (especially economic interests) first, not Cuban.

Under Magoon's supervision new elections were held in 1908, and this time José Miguel Gómez and his Liberal Party were triumphant. Indeed, the Liberals were to remain the majority party in Cuban politics until 1924. The election of 1912 brought new American intervention. Gómez, running for reelection, was opposed this time not only by Conservative Party (the inheritor of Palma's old Moderate Party) leader Mario García Menocal, but also by a group of veterans of the Revolution of 1895 who were demanding that Cuban politicians who had formerly collaborated with the Spaniards be removed from office. And, of greater significance, he was opposed also by a Negro political party, the Independent Party of Color. When the usual charges of fraud were brought and when the Party of Color was prevented from entering candidates for the election, rebellion again loomed. The United States immediately dispatched Marine reinforcements to Guantánamo and instructed the government of Gómez to arrest Party of Color leaders (which they did with alacrity). To protests, Secretary of State Philander Knox coolly replied: "The United States does not undertake first to consult the Cuban government if a crisis arises requiring a temporary landing somewhere. . . ." More U.S. Marines arrived, and the incipient rebellion was crushed by July 1912. When the elections were finally held that year García Menocal won.

By this time, of course, a fatal pattern had become evident. Elections, followed by charges of fraud, followed by rebellion, followed by United States intervention to suppress the rebellion, followed by elections, followed by. . . . For example, Menocal was reelected in 1916 while the Liberals claimed thousands of ballots had disappeared. A seven-month rebellion followed which was put down by the tireless U.S. Marines. But on that occasion the Marines stayed; not until 1922 were the last of them withdrawn.

World War I brought booming sugar prosperity to Cuba, but with the war's end and the recession of 1920-1921, the Cuban economy collapsed. In an attempt to revive it, the Cuban government (now headed by President Alfredo Zayas, a Menocal henchman) sought a $5,000,000 loan from J. P. Morgan & Company. But the U.S. State Department held up action on this private loan until the Cuban government granted American inspectors the right to inspect and audit the books of the Cuban Treasury. Although this was an unheard-of interference in the internal affairs of a supposedly sovereign nation, it was not without some justification, because the American-backed regime of Alfredo Zayas was one of the most corrupt in Cuban history. Inevitably, in 1922 yet another rebellion broke out (backed by disgruntled Liberals and veterans of the Revolution of 1895) and, inevitably, it was crushed by American interference.

By this time hatred of the United States was so profound that, for instance, on June 21, 1922, the Cuban newspaper *La Nacion* editorialized: ". . . that the day will have to arrive when we will consider it the most sacred duty of our life to walk along the street and eliminate the first American we encounter, and if at a ball to leave the side of our companion to annihilate the intruder who has for years and years annoyed us."

After 1922, for a variety of reasons the United States attempted to follow a "hands-off" policy in regard to Cuba. Among those reasons were the increasing hostility of Cubans towards Americans and American companies; a desire on the part of Republican administrations of the twenties to avoid the charge of imperialism in American domestic politics; growing opposition to American "gunboat diplomacy" on the part of other Latin American nations, and—perhaps of greatest importance—the fact that American power over Cuban affairs and American investment in the Cuban economy had now become so great that armed interference was no longer necessary: the United States could afford more subtle and quiet means of running its Caribbean plantation.

U.S. investments in Cuba increased by some 536% between 1913 and 1928. While U.S. corporations had owned about 49% of the Cuban sugar industry in 1920, they owned more than 70% of it by 1929. American interests also owned most of the cattle ranches, the tourist

50

facilities, and, with British investors, the Cuban oil industry. The scale of American investment in Cuba was neatly summed up by the U.S. Chamber of Commerce, which pointed out:

The only foreign investments of importance [in Cuba] are those of the United States. American participation exceeds 90% in the telephone and electric services, and about 50% in public service railways, and roughly 40% in raw sugar production. [*This last was a masked figure hiding U.S. control of refineries and subleasing of plantations to Cuban "front" corporations.*] The Cuban branches of United States banks are entrusted with almost one-fourth of all bank deposits. . . .

In 1924 General Gerardo Machado, a Liberal Party candidate, won the presidency by an overwhelming plurality. At first he gave the island an efficient administration—and promised repeatedly that he would not succeed himself as president. But within two years the corruption of his regime became notorious. Making use of the official government lottery, Machado bribed politicians of every political party (he himself swindled an estimated $3,000,000 per year from the lottery), suppressed opposition newspapers through terrorism (his agents murdered many a reporter and editor), rounded up and expelled from Cuba those labor leaders who could not be bought, and in 1928 not only succeeded himself as president (the opposition parties had all been bribed by him; he was unopposed), but extended his term from four to six years in defiance of the constitution.

The Great Depression in the United States brought disaster to the Cuban economy. In 1930, the enactment of the Smoot-Hawley tariff bill placed higher import duties on Cuban raw sugar, with the result that American domestic sugar importers turned to nontaxed Philippine, Puerto Rican and Hawaiian suppliers. Labor unrest in Cuba culminated in a minor rebellion in 1931 which was promptly broken by Machado's 12,000-man army. Perhaps emboldened by the revolt, the Cuban supreme court then declared the Machado regime illegal. The dictator's reply was to ban all right of appeal to the courts and institute a reign of terror. He had already organized a secret police, and this was now loosed on the country to kill thousands of Cubans

51

Fulgencio Batista

who dared to oppose his rule. With all legal means of protest denied them, Machado's enemies now organized themselves into a secret revolutionary-terrorist group called the ABC and proceeded to assasinate secret police officials and army officers. Then, in August 1933, a general strike was proclaimed by the workers of Havana which paralyzed that city and quickly spread to the countryside. The combination of ABC terrorism and the general strike proved too much for the dictator. Although he continued to enjoy U.S. support, Machado resigned (to live comfortably in exile with his stolen money).

The new provisional president, Manuel de Céspedes, was unable to win support from Cuban labor leaders and radical students or to solve the problems of Cuba's rapidly declining economy. Accordingly, on September 5, 1933, a group of noncommissioned army officers led by Sergeant Fulgencio Batista revolted and replaced Céspedes with

Ramón Grau San Martín

Ramón Grau San Martín, a much more progressive politician. Grau made some attempt to deal with his country's woes. He declared a moratorium (suspension) on the payment of Cuba's large foreign debt, passed some advanced social legislation and attempted to force the U.S.-owned Cuban utility companies to lower their rates, which were among the highest in the world. When the companies refused, Grau took over the electric plants on January 14, 1934. The reaction was instantaneous. Grau had laid hands on U.S.-owned property! The very next day, at the insistence of U.S. Ambassador Jefferson Caffrey and confronted by an ultimatum presented by Fulgencio Batista (acting as Caffrey's secular arm), Grau San Martín resigned. His administration had never been recognized by the United States—it was too independent.

After a few days of confusion Colonel Carlos Mendieta, no more than a front man for Batista, was declared president on January 24, 1934. But the workers of Havana and throughout the countryside continued to strike. The gas workers struck; the water company workers struck; the electric company workers struck; the streetcar conductors struck. Students joined the strikers, and demonstrations and riots soon followed. Batista (through his stooge, Mendieta) declared a state of siege, replaced striking workers with army troops, suspended all constitutional guarantees and shot down hundreds of workers in the strike-bound sugar mills. American response to his reign of terror was to grant the Mendieta regime a $10,000,000 credit.

In May 1934, President Franklin D. Roosevelt declared the Platt Amendment null and void, thereby relinquishing the American right of intervention in Cuban affairs, but retaining the Naval base at Guantánamo. Although Roosevelt meant this as a gesture of good will and reassurance to the Cuban people (about whom he, like every President since his cousin Teddy, was consistently, deliberately and badly misinformed by American State Department officials), it actually seemed to be a gift to the hated Batista regime. In any event, so closely allied were Batista and his henchmen with American business interests that the Platt Amendment was no longer necessary to ensure continued American control of Cuban affairs.

Making and breaking presidents as he chose (he deposed Mendieta in 1935, saw to it that another front man, Miguel Gómez, was elected in 1936, deposed Gómez in 1939 and became president himself in 1940), Batista ruled Cuba with an iron hand for ten years. During that time he enriched himself, his backers and his supposed opponents liberally from the public treasury. The Cuban government *and* its opposition became unbelievably corrupt. Under the circumstances (of graft, bribery, terror and complete army control) Batista and his cronies felt well able to throw a bone to those Cubans who sincerely and desperately longed for freedom, order and justice in their affairs. This bone was the Constitution of 1940, one of the most liberal and advanced constitutions to emerge in world history. But of course that was all on paper—and Batista himself sat in the presidential palace in Havana. Things went on as before, and Cubans groaned somewhat less under the ex-sergeant's heel, because World War II brought

Carlos Prío Socarrás

another economic boom to the island as Cuban sugar exports (and prices) skyrocketed. Then, in 1944, perhaps because he felt rich enough or had grown bored (the reasons are still unclear) Fulgencio Batista amazed everyone by observing the constitutional provision that the president must not succeed himself. He resigned his office and "retired."

The elections of 1944, which, also to everyone's surprise, were fairly honest and efficiently administered, brought Ramón Grau San Martín back to office, this time as the candidate of a new party, the Auténtico. Once again Grau proved himself personally honest and instituted some reforms, especially in the areas of cheap housing for workers and rural schools for the *guajiros*. But again Grau's associates proved themselves hopelessly corrupt; the plundering of the national wealth continued. Nonetheless, some progress had evidently been made. When new elections were held in 1948, the Auténtico Party candidate, Carlos Prío Socarrás, won easily and honestly. Prío Socarrás continued to carry out the policies of his predecessor—reform and plunder.

All during the years of the Grau and Prío Socarrás regimes, Fulgencio Batista had retained a great deal of power in Cuba. Many senators and administration officials were his creatures, and the army continued loyal to his memory. Having spent several years abroad (mainly in the United States, where he invested his plunder in Florida real estate), the ex-strong man returned to Cuba in 1952 and announced that he would be a candidate for the presidency that year under the banner of a new party, Progressive Unitary Action. His announcement was greeted with despair on the part of all those Cubans who had thought that slowly, perhaps, but surely, progress towards honest government and just administration was being made. Sensing the tragedy that was to come, Eduardo Chibás, the extremely popular leader of the Ortodoxo Party, committed suicide before the television cameras (and, hence, the eyes of millions of viewers) of station CMQ in Havana. And Chibás' forebodings proved correct. On March 10, 1952, Fulgencio Batista led the Cuban army in a seizure of power. He proclaimed himself dictator, dissolved all opposition parties, suspended the Constitution of 1940—and won immediate recognition from the United States government. Night once again descended on Cuba.

Not that it had ever really lifted for the masses of Cuban workers and *guajiros* for hundreds of years. For while the United States imposed its will on Cuba and a dreary succession of strong men and gangsters ruled the island and bickered over its plunder, the Cuban people endured a life of untold misery and degradation during which almost nothing changed except the names of their oppressors.

Cuban society in 1952 was split, as it had been for generations, between the very, very rich and the abysmally poor. It was also split between residents of Havana and all the rest of the country. In Havana there was a small middle class of shopkeepers, white-collar workers and merchants, but in the rest of Cuba this class was all but nonexistent. In Havana were the great townhouses of the very rich, the American- (largely American criminal-syndicate) run gambling casinos, the bars and nightclubs and restaurants and houses of prostitution where the easily gained plunder of a vast, corrupt government bureaucracy was spent, the thousands of shops that catered to Yankee tourists, the great hotels that housed them. In Havana, if one didn't look too closely, there was an air of bright prosperity. But even in Cuba's capital city, to which the wealth of the island poured, behind the glittering façade lay misery.

Havana's workers—industrial workers, servants to the rich, shopgirls, municipal employees—the overwhelming majority of the city's population—lived in some of the most appalling slums in the world. Only about half of all Havana's dwelling units had running water, only 40% had inside toilets, almost none had such luxuries as refrigerators. Yet rents for workers' hovels in Havana were so high that they absorbed fully half of all workers' incomes. In well-to-do neighborhoods, workers lived in *solares*—alleys lined on both sides with one-room dwellings in which several families generally lived (the alleys offering the convenience to wealthy residents of the district of having servants' quarters near their places of work). Most often more than a dozen people lived in one room, and there were rarely more than two outside toilets for a *solar* of up to two hundred people. Wages for Havana's poor were incredibly low, averaging about $180 per employed person per year. Under such circumstances children had to work, since poor families could not afford to send them to school, and in fact it was estimated that fully 25% of all Havana's children attended no school, while an even higher percentage went for only half a day. The illiteracy rate in Havana was over 12%, yet it was far and away the lowest in the country. And bad as life was for Havana's poor (the great majority of its citizens), this was the best that Cuba had to show; this was all that most American visitors ever saw.

Beyond Havana lay what the rich referred to as "the interior" (as if it were a foreign land), where life was truly miserable. More than 75% of rural Cubans lived in *bohios*—huts made from palm trees. Typically, a *bohio* had a roof made of palm leaves, walls made of palm trunks and floors of dirt. Yet those who lived in these primitive structures were at least better off than Cuba's migratory farm and sugar plantation workers. For the migratory workers most often lived in *barracones* (long sheds in which hammocks were slung) provided rent-free by the sugar companies. Still, migratory workers living in these despicable barracks were better off than the *desalojos,* Cuba's truly homeless ones. The *desalojos,* with neither *bohio* nor *barracone* to call home, simply camped inside packing crates or under newspapers by the side of the roads.

Under these circumstances it is not surprising that disease and malnutrition were rampant throughout Cuba. More than 60% of all Cuba's doctors preferred to work and live in Havana. As a result, while there was one doctor for every 420 people in Havana Province, there was but one doctor for every 2,100 people in rural Piñar del Rio and only one for every 2,550 in Oriente Province—precisely the areas where medical help was most urgently needed. Aggravating this lack of medical attention (in Cuba it was an old saying that "only the cattle are vaccinated") was the malnutrition (and, in some areas, outright starvation) induced by a poverty-imposed diet. With an average annual income per person of about $91, Cuba's peasants ate almost no meat, fish or eggs; only 11% drank milk; none ate fresh green vegetables. The *guajiro* ate rice, beans and various kinds of yams.

And if the children of Havana's poor received a scanty education, the children of the *guajiro* received much less. More than 60% of all rural children in Cuba *did not attend any school ever*—and another large percentage went only part-time and for only a few years. More than two-thirds of *all* Cubans, both urban and rural, had less than three years' schooling. Fully half of all Cuba's peasants were illiterate.

But all of this was not for lack of money in the educational system. Ever larger amounts had been appropriated by the governments of Grau and Prío Socarrás for education. Even Fulgencio Batista, of peasant background himself, had undertaken a rural education program; indeed, he had deposed President Miguel Gómez for his failure to carry out such a program. The trouble was that the money found its way into the pockets of grafters and swindlers. Many teachers sent out into the countryside continued to draw a weekly salary even though no school had as yet been organized in which they could teach. Even in the University of Havana, many professors took salaries for

58

which they did no work. Since teachers were appointed for life in Cuba, such jobs became political plums, often going to criminals and idlers. As for money appropriated to build new schools or modernize old ones, that was a very rich pork barrel for politicians and construction companies, who simply stole the tax money allocated.

Also, in the Cuban countryside, there were several aspects of life that were uniquely Cuban, different from the experience of other Latin American nations. First among these was the fact that racial discrimination was largely nonexistent among the mass of the Cuban people. Negroes and whites mingled freely and unself-consciously throughout Cuba; in fact, the existence of a large mulatto group showed what a high percentage of the population had intermarried. Cubans had many tragic problems, but one of them was not race hatred. This fact was to provide immeasurable strength for the revolutionary struggle ahead. Another odd feature of Cuban life was the lack of influence of the Catholic Church. Cubans, descendants of Spanish Catholic settlers and living within the broad framework of a Latin Catholic culture, almost never went to church and only rarely saw a priest. In all of Cuba there were not a thousand Catholic priests (there were, in fact, 700 Spanish priests and a handful of Cuban). Although professing themselves Catholic and seeing to it that their children were baptized, few Cubans (and those only a handful of the wealthy residents of Havana and other towns) paid any attention whatsoever to the teachings of their church, teachings which in any event only rarely reached them, since the Church in Cuba expressed even less interest in the people than the people did in it.

At the root of existence for most Cubans, the key to the Cuban economy and the dominant fact of Cuban life was the plantation system. The huge, sprawling sugar plantations, largely American owned, employed over half of Cuba's rural laborers. They owned about half of all the cultivable land of Cuba, and rented most of the rest. Six very large sugar companies owned nearly 60% of the sugar-cane land, and nearly half the country's sugar production was controlled by but 3% of its sugar producers.

The sugar companies did not even begin to utilize the huge areas of land they owned. They were interested only in lands capable of producing sugar. Thus, while more than 82% of Cuba's total area was cultivable, only 22% of it was planted in crops. So Cuba, with remarkably fertile soil and a subtropical climate, found herself forced to import rice, beans, fats, oils, cotton and corn to the average value of $95,000,000 per year. Not only did the sugar plantations dominate the countyside without really using it (except for sugarcane cultivation), but they also accounted for 80 to 90% of all Cuba's exports and fully one-third of the country's national income. But because sugarcane cultivation is a highly seasonal task, Cuba's plantation-bound laborers (living in their miserable "company shacks" buying their food and staples at the "company store") were unemployed for months at a time. Cuba's sugar mills operated less than six months per year. All of which meant that for long periods of each year some 30% of all Cuban workers were unemployed. And in fact, at any time from 1920 to 1952 at least 15% of the Cuban labor force was permanently out of work—a percentage reached in the United States only during the worst days of the Great Depression.

All of this misery and more (there would not be space in a book several times as long as this to chronicle the appalling wretchedness of Cuban life) was the human price paid for the exploitation of a nation by foreigners and corrupt governments under foreign control. Perhaps worst of all, the savage exploitation fed upon itself. For the great masses of the Cuban people, barely literate or illiterate, wasted by poverty and malnutrition, blighted by disease and despair, seemed unable to muster sufficient strength to change their condition. When Fulgencio Batista in 1952 proclaimed himself dictator, it appeared that most Cubans numbly accepted him as inevitable; it appeared that corrupt and dictatorial government and continued exploitation of the land and the people were Cuba's fate; it appeared that the island would always be an American economic colony, would always be the sporting ground of American tourists and gangsters; it appeared that Cuba's condition was eternal. But appearances were deceiving. . . .

4

The Twenty-Sixth of July

The man who was to prove that Cuban history could take a new direction, Fidel Castro Ruz (Ruz, being his mother's family name, followed his father's name in the Spanish tradition), was born on August 13, 1926, on his father's farm at Birán in the district of Mayarí on the north coast of Oriente Province. Fidel's father, Angel Castro, was a Galician who had come to Cuba as a soldier in the Spanish army in 1898. But when the Spanish army sailed for home after the Spanish-American War, Angel Castro decided to stay in Cuba. He went to work for the Nipe Bay Company, a subsidiary of the United Fruit Company of Boston. By 1904 he had worked his way up to be an overseer for the company, and in 1920 he sold them a particularly valuable piece of land. His wealth increased from that moment, and at his death on October 21, 1956, he was able to leave his family more than $500,000. It was said by some that Angel Castro's fortune was based on his mistreatment of *guajiros* in Oriente Province. Of course it would have been almost impossible for anyone working for the United Fruit Company *not* to mistreat local peasants in the

Fidel Castro

company's employ. But there is no evidence that Angel Castro was any harsher than he had to be. The charge seems to have sprung simply from the fact that he became rich.

Angel Castro married twice. By his second wife, Lina Ruz, he had five children: Angela, Ramón, Fidel, Raúl and Juana. Fidel and Raúl were sent to school, first to the Colegio LaSalle, a Jesuit institution, and then to the Colegio Dolores (also Jesuit). According to Fidel Castro, he and his brother were expelled from Colegio LaSalle for having organized a strike in the dining room—based on the claim that the Jesuit Fathers were showing social discrimination in the distribution of food.

In 1942, Fidel was sent to the Jesuit college of Belén in Havana. There his teachers reported that he had "good qualities, and is something of an actor." He also developed into a very good swimmer, an

62

excellent runner and a fair basketball player. He was graduated from Belén in 1945, and in the fall of that year enrolled in Havana University's Faculty of Law. The University seethed with the politics of dissent; student political associations, both open and secret, dominated the social life of the University. There the sons of the upper middle classes (a very small group in Cuba) came face to face with the corruption of Cuban governments as expressed in the low level of education available to them. While many students resented the government's corrupt domination of the University, which crippled their education for personal careers, others with wider social consciousness realized that the University was but one institution degraded by Cuban national politics. A handful of students with even wider social perceptiveness realized that the corrupt Cuban government was only one among many Latin American governments degraded by American dollar diplomacy. These students tended to see Latin American affairs as interdependent and were willing to strike a blow against dictatorship anywhere in Latin America as indirectly a blow against conditions in Cuba.

A particularly rotten and brutal dictatorship lay close at hand. This was the iron-fisted rule of General Rafael Trujillo in the nearby Dominican "Republic." In 1947 a group of Havana University students which included Fidel Castro decided to launch an invasion of the Dominican Republic to overthrow Trujillo. They received financial support from an exiled Dominican general in Cuba, Juan Rodríguez, and set out in a private motor yacht. But word of their venture leaked out, and Dominican representatives at a meeting of the Pan-American Union in Rio de Janeiro raised a howl against the government of Cuba (then headed by Grau San Martín) which forced it to take action. By that time the would-be invaders were already at sea. A Cuban navy gunboat intercepted them and they swam for shore (Fidel Castro with a tommy-gun slung around his neck) to avoid capture.

Nothing daunted by this adventure, less than a year later (in April 1948) Fidel Castro led a delegation of Cuban students to Bogotá, Colombia, to participate in an Anti-Imperialist Student Congress to be held there. The Student Congress, with student representatives from all over Latin America, had been called to protest and, hopefully, disrupt the proceedings of the Ninth Conference of the Pan-American Union (at which hemisphere foreign ministers, including American Secretary of State George C. Marshall, would be present) due to open in Bogotá on April 9. By this time Fidel had won election as president of the Law Students' Association at Havana University, so it was only natural that he head the Cuban delegation. Nor, considering conditions in Cuba, was it surprising that it was the students of Havana who had been the chief organizers of the Student Congress in Bogotá.

The Student Congress demanded, among other things, independence for Puerto Rico, the overthrow of the Trujillo dictatorship in the Dominican Republic, and Panamanian control of the Panama Canal. All of these objectives were of course primarily directed against American interests. On April 3 Fidel Castro and his group were expelled from the Colón Theater in Bogotá by the police for distributing anti-American leaflets. That didn't matter. Any publicity for their objectives, the students figured, was good publicity.

The students were not alone in opposing the Pan-American Union conference. The Liberal Party of Colombia opposed it, as did, of course, the Colombian Communist Party. But although in opposition, the Liberal Party resisted Communist attempts to sabotage the conference, and feared that the Student Congress might unwittingly fall under Communist control. Therefore a meeting was arranged between student representatives and Liberal Party leader Jorge Gaitán, one of Colombia's most important and most popular politicians. The meeting was to be held at the offices of the Liberal Party newspaper, *El Tiempo,* on April 9. But while student representatives waited, Gaitán was shot to death while walking to the meeting. The assassin was immediately beaten to death by an enraged crowd, so no one ever learned who was behind the murder.

But the Liberal Party students of Colombia and the members of the Anti-Imperialist Student Congress (as well as vast numbers of citizens of Bogotá) felt that the Colombian government was responsible. They marched on the capital, and Fidel Castro and his Cuban students joined them.

One wing of the capitol building housed a police station, and when the Liberal officer in charge heard from the crowd of Gaitán's murder he immediately started passing out weapons among them. Armed now, the angry mob burst into the capitol building itself, wrecking several rooms before hastily summoned troops expelled them. But now the students, joined by ever larger mobs, swept through the city of Bogotá like a hurricane. Buildings were set afire throughout the city; shops were looted, cars overturned, policemen beaten. The Colombian Communist Party, taking advantage of the situation, sent loudspeaker trucks roaming through the streets proclaiming the "leftist revolution of the Americas!"

The Colombian government meanwhile quickly reached an agreement with the leaders of the Liberal Party. It was obviously foolish of the students and the mobs to blame the Colombian government for the assassination of so notable a Liberal leader on the very day the foreign ministers of twenty-one American nations were due to assemble in Bogotá. In fact, addressing the nation by radio that very night, Colombian President Mariano Ospina accused the students themselves of having murdered Gaitán to create the disturbances. Although this charge was as improbable as the one hurled at the government by the students (to this day the men and causes behind Gaitán's death are unknown), popular indignation now turned against the Anti-Imperialist Student Congress. Fidel Castro and his fellow Havana University students were forced to take refuge in the Cuban Embassy. From there they were smuggled out of Colombia hidden aboard a cattle-transport airplane. The riots went into history as *"el Bogotazo"* (the "Bogotá Affair"), and Castro returned to his studies.

On October 12, 1948, Fidel Castro married a fellow student at Havana University, Mirtha Díaz Balart. The young couple spent their honeymoon in Miami—plagued by a lack of money (Fidel was still living on a small monthly allowance given him by his father). On September 1, 1949, Fidel and Mirtha celebrated the birth of their first child, a boy to be named Fidelito (little Fidel), and in 1950 Fidel finally obtained his law degree from the University. He started practicing law in Havana with two partners, but his preference for handling cases on the part of poor clients against corporations and the government kept him poor.

In the meantime, Fidel joined the Ortodoxo Party of Eduardo

Chibás which was fighting against the corruption of the government of
Prío Socarrás and winning increasing support among workers and
guajiros throughout Cuba. Castro worked energetically for the Party
and was named to run for Congress from a Havana district in the
elections which were to be held on June 1, 1952, at the end of
Prío Socarrás' term of office as president. But in December of 1952
Batista, it will be recalled, returned to Cuba and announced his
candidacy for the presidency. Shortly thereafter Chibás committed
suicide in front of the television cameras in Havana, and on March
10, 1952, Batista seized power, outlawed all political parties and
declared that there would be no more elections at all in Cuba.

Two days after Batista seized power, ex-candidate Castro appealed
to both the Emergency Court and the Court of Constitutional Guarantees in Havana. Batista, he argued, had violated specific articles of
the Cuban Constitution of 1940 which made the dictator liable to
more than one hundred years' imprisonment. He received no reply
from the Emergency Court. But the Court of Constitutional Guarantees took the trouble to reject the young lawyer's petition, declaring
that "revolution is the fount of law," and ruling that since Batista had
won power by revolutionary means, he could not therefore be considered an unconstitutional president! This fascinating interpretation
of law and of constitutional "guarantees" was to serve Castro well in
later years. In fact so neatly did it boomerang onto the Batista government that one would almost suspect collusion between Castro and the
judges, who were, in effect, legalizing in advance any revolution
which could succeed in overthrowing the Batista regime!

If the court ruling was a hint, Fidel wasted no time taking it. He
gathered around him several other members of the now-outlawed
Ortodoxo Party such as Abel Santamaría, Jesús Montañé, René
Guitart, his brother Raúl, and others and began planning action to
overthrow Batista. These "angry young men" of the Ortodoxo Party
did not, however, enjoy the complete support of the Party leaders. The
older Ortodoxo Party leaders were too timid to take part in revolutionary activity. Unlike Castro and his young followers, the Party
leaders were well known throughout Cuba and so ran a greater risk

of being tortured and killed by Batista's police (who were engaged in an orgy of repression throughout the island).

In the swanky Havana suburb of Vedado, at a house on the corner of Calle 25 and Calle O, Castro and his followers carefully thought out their plans. They determined to attack the army post at Bayamo and the army's Moncada Barracks in Santiago de Cuba. Castro foresaw two possible outcomes of the venture. If it succeeded, Batista's days of power would be numbered. If it failed, the rebels would gain a propaganda victory from their very boldness and make their cause known throughout Cuba. Santiago de Cuba was chosen as the focal point of attack because it was in Oriente Province. Oriente was Castro's home territory and that of some of his followers; they knew intimately its terrain, people and towns. Also it was one of the poorest and most oppressed rural provinces in Cuba: its long-suffering *guajiros* might be expected to aid the rebels if they were successful and hide them if they were not.

The rebels raised money to buy arms by borrowing, begging from their families and friends and, occasionally, forging checks. Arms and ammunition were secretly gathered at the farm of Ernesto Tizol in the Siboney district near Santiago where they were hidden away by Abel Santamaría and his sister Haydée. By the last week in July 1953 the rebels were ready to strike.

At three o'clock on the morning of July 26, 1953, Fidel Castro led about two hundred followers into Santiago de Cuba. The previous day had been a *fiesta* in honor of the local saint and so the streets were still crowded with celebrating citizens. Few took any particular note of a convoy of twenty-six trucks rumbling into town carrying what appeared to be regular army soldiers in the direction of the Moncada Barracks. When the convoy reached Avenida Garzón in downtown Santiago, it split into groups. Thirty men headed toward the army post at Bayamo; the other 170 continued on toward the Moncada Barracks. The 170 were already organized into subgroups with specific missions.

Raúl Castro with his group was to occupy the Palace of Justice opposite the Barracks and station men on its roof with a machine gun bearing on the Barracks. Abel Santamaría with another group was to occupy the Saturnino Lora Hospital, directly opposite the main entrance to the Barracks. Still another group was to occupy the local radio station and broadcast tapes both of Eduardo Chibás' last speech (given as he committed suicide) and of a nine-point proclamation by Fidel Castro justifying his action and outlining his plans for reshaping Cuban society—prominent among which was the promise to reestablish the Constitution of 1940. The largest group, led by Castro, was to force their way into Moncada Barracks, seize the armory and make its garrison prisoner. Obviously, much in this daring plan depended on surprise.

The small group headed by Abel Santamaría, consisting of a Doctor Muñoz, Julio Trigo, Melba Hernández, and Abel's sister Haydée (these last two dressed as nurses), penetrated the hospital without difficulty. There they prepared for their mission, which was to care for the wounded in the coming attack.

But just as the rebels prepared to assault Moncada Barracks, one of the rebel cars accidentally overturned. Moncada sentries approached to inspect it. Fidel Castro himself was forced to start shooting to distract attention from the car, and the element of surprise vanished. The time was exactly 5:15 A.M. Castro and his followers shot their way into Moncada Barracks. But once inside the large central courtyard they came under a galling fire from hastily wakened soldiers. Worse than that, it turned out that no one was really familiar with the layout of the Barracks. Instead of seizing the vital armory, the group found themselves in the barber shop! Fire onto those in the courtyard became intense. René Guitart was killed; many were wounded. Castro ordered immediate retreat. The rebels started to run, pulling off their uniforms as they went to reveal civilian clothing underneath, and hoping this would help them escape.

The rebels sought refuge in three directions. Some went to hide in the hospital occupied by Santamaría, hastily bandaging themselves and jumping into unoccupied beds to pretend they were regular patients. Others scattered to private houses in Santiago where friends might hide them. Castro and a few followers fled to the Siboney farm from where they could climb up into the wilderness of the Sierra Maestra Mountains.

Those who had hidden in the hospital were soon discovered. Army soldiers searched the place within minutes after the attack ended. At first the disguises worked; the army details were preparing to leave, satisfied that there were only sick patients in the hospital. But a hospital orderly gave the fugitives away. The soldiers grabbed all twenty of the rebels hidden there as well as the two "nurses." On the way out of the hospital a soldier killed Doctor Muñoz by shooting him through the neck.

The unlucky doctor's fate was only an earnest of what lay in store for the rebels. Batista's secret police and army reinforcements quickly descended on Santiago de Cuba. One by one those who were hiding at the houses of friends within the city were discovered. Batista's General Martín Díaz Tamayo, in charge of the operation, had orders to kill ten rebels for each soldier killed during the attack. The General carried out his instructions grimly. Prisoners discovered in Santiago were murdered "while trying to escape." Many of those held in the local prison were tortured and then murdered in their cells. Troops searching up in the Sierra Maestra for Castro himself had orders to either execute the rebels on sight or bring them, not to the local jail, but to Moncada Barracks, where presumably they would be murdered after torture. Not only did they execute, torture and murder rebels who fell into their hands, but the Batista troops conducting their house-to-house search through Santiago terrorized completely innocent citizens. So atrocious was their conduct that the Archbishop of Santiago, Monsignor Enrique Pérez, tried to intervene with General Díaz Tamayo, asking clemency. The Archbishop's plea was disregarded.

Meantime, Fidel Castro and two of his followers, exhausted and without food or ammunition, stumbled into an army patrol in the Sierra Maestra. By a stroke of incredible good luck, this particular patrol was commanded by a Lieutenant Pedro Sarria who knew Castro personally. Pretending not to recognize his prisoners, Sarria hurriedly whispered into Castro's ear telling him not to identify himself. Then, instead of shooting his prisoners or taking them to certain death at Moncada Barracks as he had been ordered to do, Sarria marched them down to Santiago and placed them in the municipal prison, where, although Castro was recognized, he was at least in the custody of local municipal police and not Batista's secret police or the army. For this action, Pedro Sarria was later to be dismissed in disgrace from the army by Batista.

Although he undoubtedly had the power, Batista neither could nor would execute all the rebels at once. Some sixty of them had been murdered after capture, but before all of them could be done away with, other factors began to weigh on the dictator's mind. First of all, it would never do to make martyrs out of all these men—that might stir up too much trouble later. Secondly, a carefully controlled trial might accomplish two objectives: it might convince Cubans that these men were no better than common criminals, and it might establish the fact that the rebellion had been financed by ex-President Prío Socarrás, then living in exile in Miami, thereby undermining Prío's popularity in Cuba and reputation for legality in the United States. Finally, the brutality of his troops in Santiago had evoked a popular outcry from the citizens there, and many of the prisoners, including Castro himself, were of very good family. Executing them out of hand would turn some very wealthy and very influential Cubans against Batista. So the dictator ordered a trial.

In preparation for the trial, General Díaz Tamayo declared that the prisoners were common criminals. Furthermore, the General explained, those who had been shot had actually been killed by Castro himself when they tried to desert their leader during the attack on Moncada Barracks! The trial, known as Case 37 on the local court docket, was set for September 21, 1953. The prisoners were meanwhile held in Boniato Prison in Santiago. When the day of trial arrived, more than one thousand Batista troops guarded the route from the prison to the Palace of Justice.

The trial quickly turned into a condemnation not of the rebels, but of the Batista government. When the public prosecutor tried to prove that the attack had been financed by ex-President Prío Socarrás, Fidel (who was acting as his own defense attorney) pulled from his pocket a detailed account of the rebel finances. He easily demonstrated that the 16,480 pesos the attack cost had all been contributed by the defendants themselves. In confusion, the public prosecutor asked for an adjournment.

When trial was resumed five days later, on September 26, Castro was not present. The police reported that he could not attend because he was "sick." At this point Melba Hernández (also a lawyer and also conducting her own defense) pulled from her hair a tightly rolled note which she handed to the president of the court. The president read aloud a message from Fidel Castro reporting that he was in excellent health but that the police were preparing to kill him "while trying to escape." The judge accepted this petition, ordered additional protection for prisoners at Boniato and asked for a medical report on Castro.

On September 28, the public prosecutor charged that the rebels had used knives to kill soldiers. But experts appointed by the court easily demonstrated that the wounds inflicted on dead soldiers were not made by knives. Then Haydée Santamaría arose and horrified the court by her testimony. She denounced the murder of Doctor Muñoz and reported the murder of at least twenty-five other rebel prisoners in the prison cells. Among those murdered had been her brother, Abel Santamaría. Haydée told how the police had brought one of her brother's eyes to her cell and asked her to avoid further torture for him by "confessing" that Prío Socarrás was behind the rebel movement. When Haydée refused to do this the police brought her Abel's other eye.

Of course the main interest in the case focused on Fidel Castro's own defense. He did not attempt to deny his leadership of the rebellion; in fact he insisted upon it. And he cited that strange decree of the Court of Constitutional Guarantees regarding the legality of a rebellion which succeeded. Unfortunately his had failed, but had he won, he pointed out, he could not have been brought to trial under the very laws the court itself had insisted on. He spoke about the murders and tortures inflicted upon his followers by the Batista secret police. He spoke about American imperialism. He spoke about unemployment among the workers and misery among the *guajiros*. He spoke about those judges still brave enough to defy the dictator. He

71

spoke about the angry middle classes and their sons, the revolutionary university students. His speech went on for hours, and when the time came for him to be sentenced, he shouted: "Condemn me! I don't care! History will absolve me!"

The court sentenced Fidel Castro and his surviving followers to fifteen years' imprisonment on the Isle of Pines, a small island off the coast which had once been the inspiration for Robert Louis Stevenson's *Treasure Island* but had long since acquired a more sinister reputation as the site of a political prison. The question has since been asked: Why did not Batista simply order the execution of Castro then and there? No complete answer is yet available. Probably many of the reasons which caused the dictator to bother with the formality of a trial in the first place also caused him to accept the relatively mild punishment decreed by the judges.

In any event, in October 1953 Fidel arrived at the Isle of Pines, where he joined his companions who had been sentenced before him. Among them was his brother Raúl, who had been condemned to thirteen years' imprisonment. Fidel's first step when he arrived at the prison was to organize a school which he named the Abel Santamaría Academy after his friend who had been tortured to death at Santiago. The program of studies consisted basically of long, rambling talks by Fidel Castro on philosophy, history and politics. But so revolutionary was Fidel's teaching that the prison authorities soon separated him from his fellow prisoners and placed him in solitary confinement.

During the two years that Castro and his followers were confined on the Isle of Pines, Batista, growing more and more assured of his absolute control of all aspects of Cuban life, lifted his press censorship and restored some constitutional guarantees—a paternal "gift" from the dictator to those of his enemies who dared to make use of it. Some Cuban newspapers printed the story of the attack on the Moncada Barracks, and years after the event, Cubans learned what had happened. They had to read a good deal between the lines, because although "free," most Cuban newspapers received regular monthly bribes from the Batista regime—as did labor leaders, teachers, lawyers, senators, opposition politicians and, of course, army officers.

Feeling a need to "legitimize" his rule (a psychological peculiarity

Raúl Castro

among twentieth-century dictators—even Hitler had kept the German Reichstag in being to rubber-stamp his decisions and provide a forum for his harangues), Batista announced that elections would be held on November 1, 1954—and of course he would be a candidate. Since an election required opposition, Batista even went so far as to provide money for his opponent, Grau San Martín, to use to electioneer. But early in the campaign it became apparent to Grau San Martín that Batista planned to "fix" the elections in any case, and he withdrew his candidacy. With no opposition Batista won handily and took up his new four-year term as president on February 24, 1955.

Since Batista's position was now doubly assured he was inclined to lend a favorable ear to those who begged an amnesty for all political prisoners (Castro and his followers were but a small percentage of the many political prisoners languishing in prisons all over the island as well as on the Isle of Pines). On May 13, 1955, the dictator announced the amnesty, and two days later Castro and his men found themselves free.

By this time, behind the stories of the corrupted press and by word of mouth, the true facts about the attack on the Moncada Barracks had become known to almost everyone in Cuba. Interest in Castro and his followers was intense. When they arrived at the Havana railway station large crowds were on hand to greet them, including many of the leaders of the Ortodoxo Party. Radio and television offers rained down on Fidel's head, but when he attempted to speak over a Havana television station a few days later, he was prevented by the government. This only confirmed Castro in an intention he had already arrived at on the Isle of Pines: he would go abroad and fight the Batista regime from exile. A few days after returning to Havana, Fidel Castro made his way to Mexico City, where Raúl and a few other Moncada veterans were already awaiting him. The exiles immediately plunged into the hard work of reestablishing a revolutionary group which was to invade Cuba and overthrow Batista. Inevitably, seeking a name for his new movement, Fidel Castro chose to call it "The Twenty-Sixth of July."

5

Mexico City to Sierra Maestra

When Fidel Castro arrived in Mexico City that summer of 1955 he had little money, no arms, few followers and no real plans—only the overriding plan of returning as soon as possible to Cuba and overthrowing the dictatorship of Fulgencio Batista. But it was in Mexico City that two very important recruits joined his "crusade"— men whose lives were to become inextricably entwined with his own and whose abilities were to have a tremendous impact on the Cuban revolutionary movement.

It was Raúl Castro who first introduced Fidel to a young Argentinian doctor who, although only twenty-seven years old, had traveled extensively throughout South America, had intimate personal knowledge of the lives of the continent's poorest peasants and Indians and had already taken part in a losing battle against American imperialism. This was Ernesto Ché Guevara, a thin, intense, handsome young man whose mental abilities and youthful outlook matched Fidel's own.

Ché Guevara was born on June 14, 1928, in the large Argentine city of Rosario. His father, Ernesto Guevara Lynch, was a civil engineer

Ernesto Ché Guevara

of Irish descent, and his mother, Celia de la Serna, was from a Spanish family. At the age of two Ché suffered his first attack of asthma—a disease which was to prove incurable in him, the fatigue and choking sensations of which were to haunt him all his life. By the age of four Ché could no longer stand the mountain climate of Rosario so the family moved to Buenos Aires. But the wet atmosphere of the Argentine capital proved no better for Ché, and the family once again moved, this time to Córdoba, where Ché's health improved. The family finally settled in Alta Gracia, a suburb of Córdoba.

Because of his disease Ché's early education was, to say the least, fitful. He could not attend school in first grade; his mother taught him to read and write. He spent second and third grades in school, but fourth, fifth and sixth grades were spent largely at home. His brothers and sisters would copy out the day's lessons for him and he

76

would do them at home under his mother's supervision. But by the time he was ready for high school Ché's health had improved sufficiently for him to travel daily to Córdoba in the tiny family auto.

A change in the family fortunes forced Ché's mother to sell the large farm they had owned at Alta Gracia and move into Córdoba. Ché had to go to work to earn spending money. By this time, through sheer willpower he had overcome his asthma to the point where he could take part in sports. At the Atalaya Athletic Club he played soccer, leaving the field from time to time to inhale from his ever present vaporizer. And he continued his studies, books being his predominant interest in life at that time.

On December 29, 1951, Ché and a school friend began a long motorcycle trip of exploration up the Pacific coast of South America. By that time Ché had been studying medicine at the University in Buenos Aires (where the family had resettled) for several years. The motorcycle trip was to be in the nature of a vacation. The two students worked their way all over South America as stevedores, porters, sailors, doctors, dishwashers—any job that would give them a chance to meet people and enough money to survive. In Peru Ché visited a leper colony in the jungle. Problems over money, passports and border regulations plagued the two students all the way, until finally, arriving penniless at Bogotá, Colombia, they were deported back to Argentina. But a collection taken up by fellow students enabled them to leave again, this time for Venezuela, where Ché left his companion to travel on to Miami, Florida. He had planned to stay only two days in Miami, but by limiting himself to eating one hamburger and drinking one cup of coffee per day he was able to stay a month, most of which time he spent reading at the Miami Public Library. When he returned to Buenos Aires Ché was called by the draft, but he was immediately rejected by the Argentine army because of his asthma.

Ché returned to the University and in March 1953 was graduated as a Doctor of Medicine. He was twenty-five and had already seen much of South America, had discovered the appalling truth about the conditions under which most of its people lived and had resolved to dedicate his life to fighting those conditions. He decided to go to Venezuela to work at the Cabo Blanco leper colony. But on his way he met an Ecuadorian lawyer who told him of the revolutionary government that had come to power in Guatemala. There really important changes were being made, and there they had need of trained and educated men. Ché immediately headed for Central America.

He arrived in Guatemala in 1954. There the popular left-wing government of President Jacobo Arbenz appointed him a medical officer in the armed forces. But Ché had been in Guatemala only a few days when the Arbenz government was overthrown by a counter-revolutionary force trained and equipped by the United States Central Intelligence Agency and backed by the United Fruit Company. The new government, a dictatorship headed by Colonel Castillo Armas, undertook savage repression—and Ché was forced to flee the country, walking and working his way north until he reached Mexico City, met Raúl Castro and learned for the first time of the Cuban revolutionary movement.

The other important recruit Fidel Castro enlisted in Mexico was Colonel Alberto Bayo, an exile from Spain who had been born in Camagüey Province in Cuba in 1892. Bayo had studied at the Infantry Academy in Spain and had fought for eleven years with the Spanish army in Morocco against Rif tribesmen. Later he had attended West Point on an exchange program and become a pilot. Back in Spain he transferred to the Spanish air force. When the Spanish Civil War broke out in 1936, Bayo elected to fight for the Republic against the Fascist rebellion led by General Francisco Franco. Being one of the few well-trained officers at the Republic's disposal, he was chosen to lead an invasion of Spain's Balearic Islands (where local officials had joined the Franco uprising). His forces were successful in their attack against the island of Ibiza, but when they landed on Mallorca, principal island of the group and a base for Italian dictator Mussolini's submarines and planes which were helping Franco, they were repulsed. Bayo continued to fight for the Republic until it collapsed in 1939. Then, like other Republican officials and officers, he made his way to Mexico and exile. Also like other Republicans, Bayo vowed he would one day return to Spain.

When Fidel and Bayo met in Mexico City in 1955, each saw in the other a means of accomplishing his own objectives. Bayo's experience, Fidel decided, was just what the Cuban insurgents needed. He could train them properly and help plan the coming invasion. On the other hand, though eager to overthrow the dictatorship that held his native island in its grip, Bayo saw the Cuban revolutionary movement as a step on his return journey to Spain. If the Cuban revolution succeeded he would have the base, the finances and the recruits he needed for the reopening of guerrilla activities against the Spanish government of Francisco Franco.

Bayo wound up his business in Mexico City and rented a farm at Chalco, beneath the shadow of the volcano of Popacatépetl. There he started training the members of the reborn Twenty-Sixth of July Movement, largely made up of veterans of the Moncada Barracks attack who had fled to Mexico and Cubans who had been exiled there earlier, but including a sprinkling of volunteers like Ché Guevara from all over South America. While the training marches through the wild and mountainous countryside of Chalco grew longer and harder, Fidel Castro (like José Martí before him) scoured Cuban communities in New York, Chicago, New Orleans and Miami for the money the revolutionaries needed.

Meanwhile, unrest back in Cuba continued to grow. The Ortodoxo Party split over the question of whether or not they were justified in engaging in armed insurrection against Batista. Fidel Castro resigned from the Party, declaring that the Cuban people were fed up with the palaver of politicians anyhow—what they were looking forward to now was action. That his view had a certain amount of justification was indicated by the sporadic armed attacks being made by small groups of desperate men (employing *Fidelista* tactics) against police stations and army posts throughout the island.

In Mexico the Mexican police stopped Castro's car one day for speeding—and discovered it to contain an arsenal of tommy guns, pistols, rifles and ammunition (Fidel was delivering them to the base at Chalco). The Mexican authorities promptly confiscated the arms and warned the Cubans that they were abusing Mexican hospitality. If this first blow was delivered accidentally, the next was not. Cuban secret agents in Mexico informed Batista of Castro's training camp. The Cuban police immediately tipped off the Mexican police—and once again the rebels' arsenal was seized. By now the rebels were fairly well trained but without equipment.

Finally, after much conniving and with the greatest difficulty, Castro was able to get arms for his men. He also managed to obtain a yacht called the *Granma* which was designed to carry ten passengers but which Fidel intended to load with eighty-two men and all their equipment. The money for the purchase of the *Granma* was supplied by Prío Socarrás' Auténtico Party, the leaders of which were in exile in Miami and plotting their own revolutionary activities in Cuba. The fact that Prío Socarrás had not financed the attack on the Moncada Barracks but did finance the *Granma* expedition is a measure of how far the "legitimate" Cuban political parties and leaders had been pushed by Batista between 1953 and 1956.

Finally, on November 25, 1956, Fidel Castro, Raúl, Ché Guevara and seventy-nine others piled aboard the *Granma* with their guns (including two antitank guns) and ammunition and set sail from the small Mexican port of Tuxpan. As soon as the little yacht hit the Gulf of Mexico everyone aboard became seasick. They sang Cuban patriotic songs for a while and searched fruitlessly for the antiseasickness tablets that were supposed to be aboard. Then they simply collapsed into the humiliating agony of nausea.

The route mapped out for the *Granma* was a wide sweep south of Cuba and around Jamaica to arrive at the town of Niquero in Oriente Province not far from Santiago de Cuba. It was planned that the *Granma* would arrive on November 30 and that *Fidelista* Frank País would organize an uprising in Santiago to coincide with the landing. But so heavily laden was the *Granma* (her twin engines laboring, failing and laboring again) that the revolutionaries were still at sea when over their radio they heard of riots at Santiago on the 30th. It was not until the early morning of December 2, 1956, that the *Granma* reached a tiny town called Belic on Las Colorados Beach south of Niquero. Because she was so overloaded, the *Granma* could not get close enough to shore, and the men had to unload her in water up to their chests. While they were doing this, disaster struck.

Batista's secret agents in Mexico had kept the dictator fairly well informed of the rebels' plans and capabilities (Ché Guevara later

claimed there was a spy among the men at Bayo's training camp). So
in a general sense the Batista forces were prepared for the invasion.
The uprising in Santiago had further alerted them and brought about
a regular army concentration in Oriente Province. Now, while Castro's
men struggled through the water with loads of arms and ammunition,
a Cuban coast guard cutter spotted them and immediately radioed
the news of their arrival to Batista headquarters. The *Granma* was
instantly abandoned (still heavily laden with much-needed supplies)
as the rebels took to their heels, making their way into a large swamp
behind the beach. No sooner had they reached it than Batista's air
force appeared overhead, fighters peeling off to strafe and bomb
everything in sight. Fortunately, by this time Fidel and his men were
plodding through dense mangrove-covered marshes and so were in-
visible from the air. There were no casualties from the air attack—but
the Batista forces were now on their trail.

Progress through the swamp was slow, delayed by one of the rebels
who had falsely claimed to know the way. Ché later wrote of this
episode: "We were . . . disoriented and walking in circles, an army of
shadows, of phantoms, walking as if moved by some obscure psychic
mechanism." There had been seven days of sickness and hunger
aboard the *Granma;* now followed three dreadful days in a swamp.
Finally, on December 5, after a night march marked by exhaustion
and near-hysteria, the rebel band reached the little town of Alegría de
Pío. By this time they had lost all their medical supplies, most of their
packs and all their guns except a few rifles and pistols and a small
amount of ammunition. A halt was ordered and the men crawled into
thickets on the edge of a dense wood, where they slept through the
morning. They paid little attention to a Piper Cub aircraft which
circled aimlessly high above them.

Then suddenly the day exploded in a hurricane of bullets that
seemed to come from all directions. Rebels began to fall, gunned
down by an unseen enemy as they rushed toward the poor cover of the
nearby cane field (the heaviest fire seemed to be coming from the
woods they'd been sleeping in). Some were killed outright; many
others, including Ché, were wounded. In the cane field Fidel desperately tried to organize his men, but it was too late. Under this baptism

of fire many abandoned their weapons and fled; others were too badly wounded to respond to orders; all were scattered into tiny groups of three or four men throughout the cane field. Amid the uproar and the screams of the dying, Camilo Cienfuegos' voice could be heard shouting: "Here no one surrenders!" Then low-flying planes joined the attack and set the cane field afire with tracer bullets. Fidel had already ordered a retreat, but now it became a rout, with small groups of men heading out of the infereno on their own. One such group of thirteen, headed by Manuel Márquez, surrendered to the army patrols who were now emerging from the woods, on the promise that their lives would be spared. But no sooner had they thrown down their weapons than they were all gunned down.

Raúl Castro emerged from the cane field with only three followers. They wandered for a week through the region without food or drink. Ché Guevara and four others were equally adrift. Fidel Castro himself was left with no weapons and but two companions. And these twelve men were all who remained from the eighty-two who had landed just a few days before at Belic.

The groups wandered through the countryside for days without establishing contact with each other. In fact they didn't even know whether anyone outside their particular group was still alive. They slept in caves and swamps, ate land crabs and sugarcane, scooped water from hollowed rocks and bandaged their wounds as best they could with palm leaves and mud. They were badly demoralized; probably only the certain death awaiting them at the hands of Batista's soldiers prevented some of them from surrendering. After wandering for a few days, Ché and his followers literally stumbled into Raúl Castro's group. Together the tiny band staggered on. They were afraid to approach peasant houses in the district for fear of betrayal, and time and again they only barely avoided running into army patrols.

Then one day, from their temporary "camp" atop a hill, the rebel band spotted what appeared to be an army patrol atop the next hill. They could not turn back, for they knew that Batista forces were on their trail—and now they could not go forward either. For two days the rebels eyed the forces on the hill before them. Then a local *guajiro* stumbled into their camp. He insisted there were no army units in the immediate vicinity, and that the "army patrol" on the next hill was actually a tiny band of rebels. Raúl refused to believe the peasant at first. But finally, after a very cautious patrol, they learned that the *guajiro* had spoken the truth. Atop the next hill had been Fidel Castro himself and his two companions—and each group of rebels had been sure the other was an army unit! It was in this way that the small band of survivors from the disaster at Alegría de Pío joined together again.

Their rejoicing was sobered by the knowledge that they were the *only* survivors, and also by a rebuke administered by Fidel. Learning that some of the men had abandoned their weapons during their agonized journey, he said: "You have not paid for the error you committed, because the price you pay for the abandonment of your weapons under such circumstances is your life. The one and only hope you would have had of survival, in the event of a head-on encounter with the army, was your guns. To abandon them was criminal and stupid."

But this was not the only lesson taught by defeat. It was now understood that army planes had been able to spot the fugitives when they lit campfires to cook. And army patrols had followed their paths by the shavings left behind when they cut down sugarcane to eat. But far and away the greatest danger they had faced lay in betrayal by local *guajiros*. Large army forces were everywhere in the province, and the peasants were terrified. They had every right to be. Army patrols murdered peasants and their families on the slightest pretext, even if they only suspected that rebels had been anywhere in the vicinity. The smoke from burning *bohios* arose against every horizon. Under the circumstances it was expecting very much indeed to hope that *guajiros* would not inform army units when the rebels were nearby. And even those *guajiros* who were prepared to help them could not necessarily be expected to keep their mouths shut—the news that Fidel Castro and his men were close by was too weighty a secret. One *guajiro* would entrust the information to another who would tell only his closest friend who would in turn tell someone else, until inevitably the news reached an informer.

The only rebel hope for survival lay in reaching the high peaks of the rugged Sierra Maestra, and it was there that Fidel led them. After

83

a terribly hard journey (hiding by day, scrambling up the rocks by night), on Christmas Day, 1956, Fidel Castro and his eleven followers reached the top of Pico Turquino, the highest mountain in Cuba. "The first thing I did on reaching the top," Castro was later to recall, "was to prove that the height given in Cuban geography books was more than fifty meters out according to my altimeter." But there were more pressing problems than geography. Survival was the foremost.

The Sierra Maestra has an area of about 1,500 square miles and a population of about 50,000—mostly *guajiros*. It is a region of jungle-covered mountains where sugarcane, coffee and tobacco grow wild. In those days it had no communications, no roads better than trails, no hospitals, no doctors, no schools—and no government officials. The *guajiros* there had long since been abandoned to disease, starvation, illiteracy and despair by a succession of Cuban governments. Their only contact with Havana was the appearance of an occasional army patrol—signalized by looting, rapes and murders. If Fidel Castro's revolution was to survive it would have to win the confidence and help of the *guajiros* of the Sierra Maestra. Two factors enabled Fidel to accomplish this.

The first was simply good luck. Throughout the Sierra Maestra a huge white-haired bearded giant named Crescencio Pérez was The Law. Always armed with a Colt .45, "married" to three different women at once, Pérez was the unofficial judge, sheriff, counselor and "father" to the *guajiros,* who trusted him implicitly. And Crescencio Pérez had long hated the Batista regime, had even organized unsuccessful uprisings against it. As soon as Castro reappeared in Cuba, Pérez had decided he would follow him; now, in the Sierra Maestra, he joined the rebel forces.

The other factor that brought Castro *guajiro* support was not accidental, but carefully thought out. Fidel was an omnivorous reader, and by this time he had read almost all the classic texts of revolutions from Russia to China. He was perfectly aware of the necessity of a revolutionary army's drawing its strength from the people, familiar with Mao Tse-tung's maxim: "The people are like the water and the revolutionary forces are like fishes who must swim in the water." His study of the experience of other revolutions only reinforced his natural inclinations, which were to treat the *guajiros* as well as possible. Accordingly, Castro's men always paid for everything they ate. They kept away from hamlets and *bohios* when army troops were in the vicinity so as not to endanger *guajiros* by their presence. Ché's medical knowledge and small medical supplies were used to cure *guajiros* suffering from disease whenever possible. And *guajiros* were reassured by Castro's firm policy of executing landowners who betrayed *guajiros* suspected of aiding the rebel cause. In fact his second act after reaching the top of Pico Turquino (his first having been to glance at his altimeter) was to order the execution of a captured landowner for denouncing some *guajiros* who as a result had been shot by the army for "harboring criminals."

These policies, plus the help of Crescencio Pérez, gradually brought to Castro's side the overwhelming majority of the impoverished inhabitants of the Sierra Maestra. And this was of incalculable importance. *Guajiros* acted as spies for Castro, but refused information or lied to army units. *Guajiros* could be counted on to hide *Fidelistas* in their *bohios* and to care for the wounded left behind after an attack. They could be counted on to relay messages all over the mountains and to establish contact with towns on the plains below. It became possible for Castro to set up caches of food and ammunition at various strategic points in the Sierra, thereby enabling his men to travel unhampered by heavy loads, to move fast, confident that supplies awaited them within a twenty-four-hour march in almost any direction. And, of very great importance, fighting recruits could be drawn from the peasant population. Although they had no arms, in fact had never handled a rifle or a pistol in their lives, they were hardy and quick to learn. Above all, they were driven by despair behind and lured by hope in front; many were to make excellent soldiers.

While Castro was consolidating his position in the Sierra Maestra, Batista's controlled press and radio in Havana were announcing the extermination of the rebel leader and all his men. First it was claimed they had all died on the beach at Belic. Then it was reported they had all been wiped out at the battle of Alegría de Pío. Next it was revealed that their bodies had been discovered scattered along the trails and in the swamps below the mountains. And although few

Cubans placed much reliance on their government's information, few knew for certain that these claims were untrue. It was certainly true that the rebels had suffered disaster—but had they really all been killed? Was Fidel Castro dead and this Twenty-Sixth of July Movement suppressed? All sorts of rumors were coming out of the Sierra Maestra—but the people were uncertain.

It was for this reason that Castro saw his first objective as that of undertaking some action which would prove his continued existence and the continuing determination of his Movement. There were two ways in which this could be accomplished. First, a neutral newsman might somehow be smuggled past the army lines into the Sierra Maestra; second, a successful attack on an army post would certainly crack through Batista's censorship barrier. Making use of *guajiros* to carry messages to trusted undercover agents in Santiago and Havana, Castro asked for the newsman. And to accomplish his second objective he prepared to attack the army barracks at the mouth of the La Plata River in the Sierra Maestra.

This attack at La Plata was a terribly risky undertaking. Although a few recruits had made their way to join the rebels, their numbers were still small; they were poorly armed (they had only twenty-three usable weapons, including a sawed-off shotgun), and they had little ammunition. This last was most serious. Unless they were able to capture the army post and replenish their supply of ammunition after the battle from captured stores, they would be in effect disarmed. Castro's men *had* to win the battle of La Plata.

On January 15 the little band of rebels, after a long and gruelling march, reached a jungle-covered hill above their objective, the half-finished zinc-roofed army barracks standing next to the river where it met the sea. Two passing (and badly frightened) *guajiros* informed the rebels that there were fifteen soldiers stationed there. Furthermore, they passed along the interesting information that one of the most notoriously cruel and corrupt overseers in the region, a certain Chicho Osorio, would soon be passing by.

The rebels hid in the brush, and when Osorio appeared they ordered him to halt in the name of the *Guardia Rural*. The *Guardia Rural* was a local militia force in Oriente Province composed of

86

guajiros and plantation foremen—any who either had nothing better to do or enjoyed terrorizing the peasants. It was poorly equipped and generally raggedly clothed. So when Castro's men announced to Osorio that they were *"Rurales,"* he took one look at them and believed them. Their imposture was also helped by the fact that Osorio was roaring drunk. He boasted of how he had helped kill a *Fidelista* prisoner not long before—thereby signing his own death warrant. Fidel Castro now appeared and told Osorio that he was an army colonel who was empowered to find out why army posts in the Sierra Maestra displayed such lax discipline. At Castro's suggestion, the drunken Osorio agreed to lead the rebels to the barracks below to surprise the troops there and prove to them how unprepared and neglectful they were of their duties.

With Osorio as a guide, the little band made its way down the hillside to within a few yards of the barracks. The time was 2:40 A.M., and they could see the glow of the sentry's cigarette as he paced back and forth in the pitch blackness. Suddenly Fidel Castro opened up with his submachine gun. Immediately everybody started shooting at once. Both the sentry and Osorio were killed and the barracks was riddled by bullets. Castro called out to the soldiers within to surrender. Their reply was to open fire with M-1 rifles. So heavy was the hail of bullets that it appeared the battle might be a standoff.

Castro ordered two of his followers to throw their old-fashioned Brazilian hand grenades at the building. The grenades failed to explode. Then Raúl Castro threw a few sticks of dynamite. These also failed to explode. Finally Ché Guevara and Luis Crespo inched their way over to the building, crawling on their stomachs beneath a hail of lead, and set fire to it. Almost immediately soldiers began running from the burning barracks—to be cut down by rebel fire outside. The troops suffered five casualties and then surrendered. But in the darkness many escaped, leaving Castro with but three prisoners aside from the wounded and the dead.

It was not prisoners in which Castro was interested, however. Hastily the rebels (who had not suffered a scratch in the fighting) counted their booty: eight Springfield rifles, a Thompson submachine gun and, most precious of all, one thousand rounds of ammunition.

Counting up, they found they had expended five hundred rounds during the battle, so their supply was now doubled. The rebels set fire to several smaller buildings around the barracks, left the wounded soldiers in the care of the prisoners and withdrew, quickly, quietly—as though they had never been there. Soon they were back in their mountain fastness.

The news of the victory at La Plata could not be suppressed even by Batista's stringent censorship. It had obviously not been won by ghosts. Although Batista's propagandists kept insisting that Castro was dead and his rebel band nonexistent, most Cubans were now convinced that the dictator was lying. The attack on La Plata therefore achieved its primary purpose.

But if any Cubans (or people anywhere else) still entertained doubts about Castro's existence or the existence of armed resistance to Batista in the Sierra Maestra, or the seriousness of the rebels' purpose, these doubts were laid to rest by the arrival of the journalist Castro had invited before the battle of La Plata.

Castro's *guajiro* messengers and undercover agents in Santiago and Havana had served him well. For the journalist they delivered (passing him right through the army lines, guided by Haydée Santamaría) was none other than Herbert L. Matthews, one of the most famous and highly respected correspondents of the prestigious *New York Times*. Batista was going to look foolish trying to deny anything that a man of Matthews' stature wrote. The American journalist had flown from New York to Havana and had then been conducted by way of Santiago to the Sierra Maestra. He found himself in the rebel camp and face to face with Fidel Castro on February 14, 1957. After hours of talking to the rebels, and especially to Fidel, and taking pictures with a little box Brownie camera he had brought, Matthews left—to follow the same risky trail back through army lines to Santiago, then on to Havana and New York. Within a few days the *New York Times* printed Matthews' article. When Batista still insisted on denying that the American correspondent could possibly have talked to the "dead" Fidel Castro, Matthews published another article—this time with pictures.

The importance of this episode lay not, however, in the humilia-

Herbert L. Matthews.

tion of the Cuban dictator. Nor was it only important because it reassured the Cuban people once and for all that Castro was "alive and well in the Sierra Maestra." Its real significance was that it aroused the interest of the entire world. Castro, who had been all but unknown before, was now a world celebrity. His almost legendary escapades and the devotion and bravery of the tiny band of men who followed him aroused passionate excitement everywhere. And if most were struck by the romantic adventurousness of his activities, there were many who were impressed by his objectives. The small but brutal war in the Sierra Maestra now attracted worldwide attention to conditions throughout Cuba under the heel of the Batista tyranny. As the dictator's repressions, political trials, extermination campaigns and murders became front-page news, an important wave of sympathy went out from most readers to the Twenty-Sixth of July Movement and its legendary leader. The sympathy (especially in North America) was important not only because it emboldened Cubans both in exile and at home to help Castro, but also because it forced Batista, worried now about a cutoff in the flow of American arms and ammunition which he had been receiving, to act with greater caution and circumspection. The arrests, tortures and murders would continue, but now there was a necessity that they be carried out secretly—and hence, less efficiently.

But for Fidel Castro and his men, outside sympathy, though gratifying, could not immediately solve their very real and desperate problems; how to eat; how to get more guns and ammunition; how to gather recruits; how to evade the increasing number of army patrols that now ascended into the mountains; where to strike next. Ahead of them, as they well knew, lay a long and bitter campaign.

6

Sierra Maestra to Havana

That famous newspaper article by Herbert L. Matthews had yet
another result. It caused Batista to send heavy army reinforcements
to the Sierra Maestra and to put a price of 100,000 pesos on Fidel
Castro's head—a sum that more than one man tried to collect. From
the very beginning the rebel forces had been plagued by informers,
traitors and spies. Small as their group was, it took only one such
person to bring ruin. Time and again Castro's men walked into army
ambushes or were bombed and strafed from the air by surprise. At
first the rebels could not figure out how their presence could be so
quickly discovered or their route of march known. Like other revolutionaries in history (for example, the American revolutionists in 1778)
they were not quick to suspect of treachery comrades in arms who
marched with them, suffered with them, fought with them. Desertions,
yes—the *guajiros* or volunteers from the plains (sent out by rebel
underground groups in Havana or Santiago) would sometimes decide
that the rough life of the Sierra Maestra *guerrilleros* was not for them.
Such men would sometimes slip away during the night or during the

heat of battle. But the information such deserters carried was slight. Castro almost never revealed his next objective or the routes of march to his followers until the last possible minute. This sort of information was known only to Fidel's closest supporters, such as Raúl, Ché and Crescencio Pérez. But on a few occasions, especially at the beginning of the struggle, intimate associates of Castro betrayed him. One such was Eutimio Guerra, a peasant who had early joined the rebel band and who had even guided it to the victory at La Plata. But it was not long after that battle that the rebels began to notice that every time Eutimio took a few days' leave (to "visit his sick mother," for example) or went on a solitary reconnaissance mission, his absence would be followed by a surprise ambush or a heavy air attack. Proof that the man was a traitor did not become positive, however, until the time of Matthews' visit—which occurred during one of Eutimio's absences from the rebel camp. Shortly after Matthews departed, a rebel patrol caught Eutimio Guerra—and he was carrying three grenades and a safe conduct from the army commander in Oriente Province. Ché Guevara has left a description of what happened next:

> Once captured and this incriminating evidence discovered, he could not doubt his fate. He fell on his knees before Fidel and asked simply that we kill him. He said he knew he deserved death. At that moment he seemed to have aged; on his temple were a good many gray hairs we had never noticed before.
> The moment was one of extraordinary tension. Fidel upbraided him harshly for his betrayal and Eutimio wanted only to be shot, for he recognized his guilt. We can never forget the moment Ciro Frías, a close friend of his, began to speak to him; he reminded Eutimio of everything he had done for him, of the little favors he and his brother had done for Eutimio's family, and of how Eutimio had betrayed them, first by causing the death of Ciro's brother—whom Eutimio had turned over to the army—and then by trying to destroy the whole group. It was a long and moving speech, which Eutimio listened to in silence, his head bent. We asked him if he wanted anything and he answered yes, that he wanted the Revolution, or rather us, to take care of his children.
>
> The Revolution has kept this promise. . . .
> Just then a heavy storm broke and the sky darkened; in the midst

of a deluge, when the sky was crossed by lightning and there was the noise of thunder, as one of these strokes of lightning burst and was followed closely by a thunderbolt, Eutimio Guerra's life was ended. Even those comrades standing near him did not hear the shot.

The death of a traitor (there would be others), the exhausting night march, the miserable food (often snakes and roots), the attacks on tiny isolated army posts, the agony of the wounded (for whom there were but few medical supplies) and the stunned, surprised expressions of the dead, the desperate search for arms and ammunition, the tortuous chain of "reliables" who could forward information from the cities, the slow trickle of arms smuggled up to the mountains and the even slower trickle of men making their way individually, sometimes in small groups, from the plains to join the *Fidelistas*: this was the daily life of the Revolution. But by March of 1957 it became apparent that the Revolution did not exist only in the mountain fastnesses of Oriente Province, but was spreading throughout Cuba. Nor were all of the revolutionary groups that began to sprout, under Castro's command.

There was, for example, the Revolutionary Directorate—a group of Havana University students with no connection at all to the Twenty-Sixth of July Movement. These young men planned a desperate stroke: they would assassinate Batista and attempt a direct takeover of power in Havana. Accordingly, on March 13, 1957, at three in the afternoon (the Cuban *siesta* hour), a truck pulled up before the Presidential Palace in Havana. A group of armed men jumped out of it and shot their way past the Palace sentries, taking everyone by surprise and rushing into the Palace. But when the gunmen reached Batista's first-floor office they found that the dictator had left it. He was suffering from a headache and had retired to his personal apartment on the second floor. In only a matter of minutes the entire Palace guard had poured out of their quarters and charged into the Palace, machine-gunning everyone in sight. Twenty-five of the student rebels were shot down and the rest had to surrender. Many of them would be executed or murdered later.

On one of the dead students the police discovered a paper bearing the name of Dr. Pelayo Cuervo, a famous Havana lawyer. That was all—just the name, no indication that Dr. Cuervo was in any way associated with the attempted uprising. This, however, was sufficient for the Batista police. They sent out two squad cars (called *persegui-dores* by Cubans), ran down Dr. Cuervo, took him to the edge of a small pond in Havana and shot him dead. This murder of one of Havana's most respected citizens aroused a storm of popular protest. Dr. Cuervo had been a member of the Cuban "establishment." His brutal murder made it clear to even the most conservative Cubans of the upper classes that Batista's dictatorship threatened them just as much as it threatened workers and peasants. Rich Cubans who had supported Batista as a means of enforcing "law and order" on their rebellious "lower classes" now began to learn the same lesson learned in Nazi concentration camps by those wealthy Germans who had supported Hitler's rise to power: fascism devours itself and its supporters as readily as its enemies, and a dictator once established will act in no one's interests but his own.

Repression in Havana and Santiago (with Batista's police murdering "suspects," machine-gunning people from speeding cars in the public streets, throwing people into prison on the slightest provocation) drove more and more young men to make the terribly dangerous trip from the cities up to the Sierra Maestra to join Castro's bands. The group had now split into three tiny subgroups headed by Fidel, Raúl and Ché Guevara respectively; another, headed by Camilo Cienfuegos, would soon appear. But Castro was embarrassed by a continuing lack of arms. Those volunteers who came to him without guns had to be turned away—to be told they would be accepted for the rebel army only when they returned with a rifle or other weapon. As a result, individual Batista soldiers throughout Cuba began to fall victim to men who would attack and often kill them just for their weapons. Tension on the island mounted. Armando Hart, underground leader of the Twenty-Sixth of July Movement in Havana, was captured by police. But as he was being led off to jail he managed to slip away from his captors— leaving them holding his empty jacket! Hart made good his escape, arriving shortly afterward at Castro's headquarters in the Sierra Maestra.

Also arriving at Castro's mountain camp at this time were three young Americans, teen-agers who had run away from their families at the Guantánamo Naval Base to join the Twenty-Sixth of July Movement. Recognizing that their motives were not so much revolutionary as simply a youthful desire for adventure, and that they were not tough enough to stand the meager rations, gruelling marches and unhealthy climate of the Sierra, Castro soon managed to ship them off to Santiago, from where they were taken back to Guantánamo. Unimportant in itself, the incident earned Castro widespread (and favorable) publicity in the North American press.

In April 1957 a new batch of *guerrilleros* was dispatched to Cuba from Mexico by General Bayo, whose training camp at Chalco, though under close observation by Mexican police, continued functioning. These men—there were twenty-seven of them—embarked aboard the yacht *Corintia* and succeeded in landing near the foothills of the Sierra de Cristal (where their presence, it was hoped, would relieve pressure on Castro's forces in the Sierra Maestra). But the group was almost immediately set upon by regular army forces. Only ten men got away (to join underground groups in nearby towns), the rest were executed as soon as they surrendered. But if this attempt to set up a "second front" ended in disaster, *Fidelista* agents in Havana and Santiago did manage to send Castro reinforcements and arms in increasing quantities. By April his band numbered about eighty men.

On May 27, after weeks spent marching to toughen up the new recruits (some of whom, not showing sufficient spirit or strength, were dismissed from the group), Castro and his followers fell upon the army post at El Uvero. It was a well-staffed post with more than fifty soldiers stationed in a lumber camp. The battle followed the pattern of that at La Plata—Castro's men dividing into squads, each with specifically assigned tasks. Three squads were directed to capture the two guard posts, two other squads were sent to cut off the roads into El Uvero to stop reinforcements, while the remaining men rained bullets on the central barracks. If it followed the same pattern, the battle of El Uvero was also bloodier. In two hours and forty-five minutes six rebels were killed and many more wounded, while army casualties were double that number. Again, as soon as the post surrendered the wounded were gathered together, given what first aid Ché could supply and left in the care of the army prisoners—while the rebel bands vanished back into the jungle, and eventually up into the Sierra.

And this was the pattern the Revolution now took—isolated, widely scattered attacks upon army posts in the Sierra, which forced Batista eventually to pull back his troops completely out of the mountains. These attacks took a much larger toll of army morale than of army personnel. Regular army soldiers stationed anywhere in Oriente Province began to look over their shoulders as they paraded their sentry posts, began to show their apprehension by shirking patrols. The mountains were high and the jungle deep—and the rebel bands might be anywhere, might strike from any direction at any time. They never offered open battle but always struck by surprise and then vanished. And combined with this continuing assault upon army strength and nerves was a progressive pattern of sabotage on the plains below the Sierra and in the big cities. In June 1957, for example, a band of Twenty-Sixth of July men blew up some high-tension transformers outside Havana that cut off the city's light for fifty hours.

There were other signs and portents. For example, in June a Catholic priest—one Father Guillermo Sardiñas—ascended into the Sierra to join Castro's men. Among religious Cubans this was a propaganda victory for Castro. Of greater importance and a much more ominous sign for Batista was that just about the time Father Sardiñas was clambering up into the mountains, the United States ambassador in Havana, Arthur Gardner, long an avowed Batista supporter, was replaced by Earl T. Smith, who pointedly refused to identify himself with the government of the Cuban dictator.

On July 31, 1957, Earl Smith made a visit to Santiago de Cuba. He found himself in a city in mourning. Only two days before, a young schoolmaster named Frank País had been killed by the Santiago chief of police. Frank País had long been a leading member of the Twenty-Sixth of July underground in Cuba. It was he who had organized the uprising in Santiago that was supposed to coincide with the arrival of the *Granma* on November 30, 1956. The uprising had been brutally

ABOVE: *The Admiral of* The Ocean Sea *is greeted by demure Cuban Indians in this very old engraving.*

BELOW: *The rebellions of the nineteenth century were often put down with ferocious cruelty by regular Spanish Army forces.*

OPPOSITE ABOVE: *The U.S. battleship* Maine *goes to her watery grave in Havana harbor.*

OPPOSITE BELOW: *"Teddy" Roosevelt leads his Rough Riders up San Juan Hill—the only trouble being that, despite this print, they actually* walked *up—and cautiously.*

BELOW: *General Leonard Wood, U.S.A. (seated at right in pith helmet), watches a volunteer being inoculated against Yellow Fever—wiped out by U.S. occupying forces in Cuba.*

OPPOSITE: *For wealthy Cubans and American tourists, Havana's night life was luxurious and gay—though dominated, as was this gambling casino, by American gangsters.*

ABOVE: *The stark reality of life in rural Cuba: crushingly heavy work in the sugar cane fields of the nation's one-crop economy.*

OPPOSITE ABOVE: *Fidel and Raul Castro discuss their next steps during early days in the Sierra Maestra.*

OPPOSITE BELOW: New York Times *correspondent Herbert L. Matthews made his way past Batista's blockade of Oriente Province to interview Castro.*

BELOW: *Ché Guevara and his men relax after battle in the Sierra Maestra.*

Victory! Fidel Castro's triumphant entry into Havana, January, 1959.

ABOVE: *Former Batista henchmen entering Havana's sports stadium to face a mass war-crimes trial. At far right stands Major Jesus Sosa Blanco.*

BELOW: *Castro speaks with moderation and dignity before the United Nations.*

ABOVE: *Invasion wreckage litters the Bay of Pigs—mute testimony to an old adage: "Those who will not learn history are condemned to repeat it."*

BELOW: *The U.S. Navy inspects a Soviet freighter during the tense period of quarantine imposed on Cuba as a result of the missile crisis.*

Behind them a billboard celebrating Castro's victory at the Bay of Pigs, Cuban students drill to be ready for any future emergency.

ABOVE: *The fate of more than a few homes of wealthy Cubans—converted into schools for the people.*

BELOW: *Castro's militia doubles in brass on a Havana street.*

ABOVE: *Russian technicians seem incongruously out of place in Havana's tropical elegance.*

BELOW: *Russian aid to Cuba (here, a new hospital) has been generous.*

651 CAMAS
EQUIPO MEDICO
Donado por la
UNION SOVIETICA

The American presence is as old as independent Cuba. Quitting time for Cuban workers at Guantánamo Bay.

There is no doubt, despite the Russian and Chinese presence, who runs Cuba.

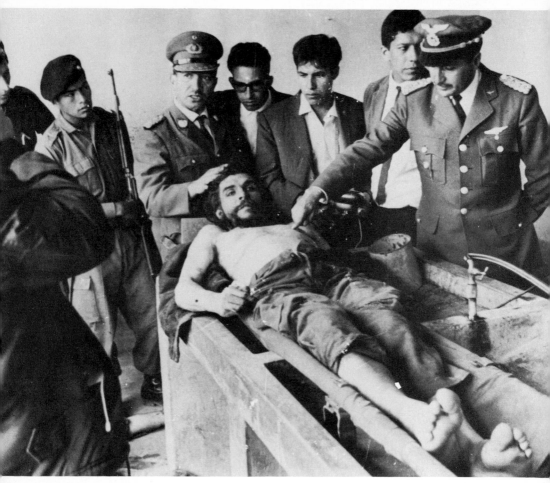

End of a revolutionary. Bolivian Army officers display the body of their murdered prisoner, Ché Guevara.

repressed, but the leaders had not been caught. Then, in June 1957, José País, Frank's younger brother, had been captured by the police and executed. One month later they caught up with Frank and killed him too. Fidel Castro sent orders from the Sierra that Frank País was to be buried as a colonel in the Twenty-Sixth of July Movement—a rank attained by no one else in the history of the Movement, not even Castro himself, who remained a major. It was the day following this burial that the new American ambassador alighted from his car in Santiago to find himself facing a huge crowd of women begging him to intervene to put an end to the police executions. As the American ambassador watched, horrified, the police charged the crowd of women brutally. A few hours later—as soon as he could summon a press conference—the American ambassador made a ringing denunciation of police brutality in Cuba. And this was not only a propaganda victory for Castro; it was also a blow for better Cuban-American relations. Earl Smith became the first American ambassador in many, many years to win the respect and sympathy of the Cuban people. Unfortunately, this new goodwill was somewhat eroded a few days later when the Pentagon dispatched a general to present the U.S. Legion of Merit decoration to Colonel Carlos Tabernilla, chief of Batista's air force and the man who had so brutally put down the Santiago uprising.

After the battle of El Uvero, a new guerrilla tactic was adopted by the rebels in the Sierra. They would henceforth attack army posts not so much to destroy them as to lure reinforcements into ambushes. This method was tried out at the battle of Pino del Agua and proved a resounding success: enough firepower was laid down on the barracks to make sure they sent out frantic appeals for help. Then another rebel group ambushed the reinforcements, inflicting a far heavier blow than merely the destruction of the army post itself.

Also after El Uvero, the rebel command was divided, with Fidel Castro leading the main column while Ché Guevara led another. As more and more volunteers reached the Sierra it was possible to establish two additional columns, one commanded by Raúl Castro and another under Juan Almeida. The groups, it will be seen, were kept small; whenever Fidel's Column Number One grew too large, new

97

columns would be split off from it. This increased guerrilla mobility, and also guerrilla "presence," in the Sierra. Simultaneous attacks by widely separated columns gave the impression that the entire Sierra was full of rebel bands. Nor was this impression very much exaggerated. By the end of 1957 the Twenty-Sixth of July men had effectively consolidated their control of the entire Sierra Maestra. Batista's forces could no longer penetrate this wilderness unless they came in great strength, and when they did that, they could not maneuver quickly and their clumsy columns were time and again ambushed by guerrilla bands. By the beginning of 1958 regular army forces rarely left the lowlands of Oriente Province. On the other hand, if the guerrillas were now supreme in the mountains, they were not yet strong enough to successfully do more than carry out minor raids against the strongly fortified Batista army encampments on the plains. A short period of stalemate developed between the opposing forces.

Meanwhile, sporadic outbreaks of anti-Batista activity continued to flare up throughout Cuba. Small guerrilla bands, copying *Fidelista* tactics, established themselves in the Sierra de Escambray, the Sierra de Cristal and the Sierra de Baracoa. Some of these were effective, some were not. Some were in touch with the Twenty-Sixth of July Movement, others were controlled by the Student Directorate or vaguely backed by Prío Socarrás from Miami. One incident, more notable for the light it sheds on the nature of all revolutions than for results, was the uprising at Cienfuegos Naval Base on September 5, 1957.

A student of revolutions might have predicted the Cienfuegos uprising. In the history of every revolution some such attempt has been made. The lower echelons of the ruling class, especially the military, foreseeing the success of a people's revolution and fearing that it will go much further in radicalizing society than would be acceptable, seek to forestall the revolution by a rebellion which will remove the figureheads of government and yet secure continued control of the nation for the "establishment." The French Revolution witnessed the "liberal" Marquis de Lafayette's rebellion against the decaying monarchy of Louis XVI; the Russian Revolution witnessed various plots on the part of aristocrats and "liberal" officials against the tzar which culminated in the murder of Nicholas II's closest advisor, Rasputin; the Chinese Revolution of Sun Yat-sen was momentarily forestalled by a successful seizure of power from the dissolving Manchu Dynasty by "liberal" General Yuan Shu-kai in 1912.

The Cienfuegos uprising was to have been part of a nationwide rebellion carried out by the military. Castro's followers today charge that it was permeated by "Yankee imperialism." If this is not true, it should have been true. American conservatives with interests in Cuba ought to have been able to predict the eventual outcome of Castro's revolution and ought to have been smart enough to attempt to forestall it by backing a more conservative revolution. (To expect such conservative American elements to display sufficient intelligence to realize that any such attempt, even if successful, could not hope to long delay the real Cuban Revolution would be expecting too much—as the history of the Bay of Pigs fiasco was to demonstrate.)

In any event, something went wrong. Cienfuegos rose before the rest of the military bases were ready. Isolated, this rebellion, led in Cienfuegos itself by Naval Lieutenant José San Román Toledo, was quickly and brutally suppressed by Batista. The people of Cienfuegos (including various Twenty-Sixth of July leaders) supported the Naval officers—and shared in the general disaster. Hundreds were murdered, hundreds more jailed and later executed. José San Román Toledo himself was carried off to Havana, where he was tortured to death.

Meantime the grim business of destroying Batista's government continued to be primarily directed from the lonely fastnesses of the Sierra Maestra. In January 1958 Fidel Castro ordered his followers to begin burning down sugar plantations with the object of weakening the Cuban economy. In order to set an example, he ordered that this harsh measure begin with the burning of those sugar plantations which belonged to his own family. But this measure proved too unpopular with the *guajiros* to be continued. Burning the sugar plantations deprived them of jobs, their only income, their food. It was quickly discontinued.

Ché Guevara's column was assigned the task of setting up a secure base in a remote valley of the Sierra. Early in 1958 the base was operating. It had a hospital, a prisoner-of-war camp (from now on prisoners could be kept, rather than released), a rude clothing factory, a small printing press which ground out a one-page newspaper and countless pamphlets, and even an armory where weapons could be repaired, adapted, and in some cases manufactured. One of the most famous weapons made there was a device thought up by Ché himself which he ominously called the M-26-7. It was nothing more than a metal tube made out of the corrugated iron *guajiros* sometimes used to roof their *bohios*. It was packed with stones and bits of metal and fired by a charge of gunpowder in its base. It could really hurt no one. But the noise it made sounded just like that of an 81-millimeter mortar, and it terrified Batista's troops on more than one occasion.

The increasing strength of the guerrilla movement in the Sierra was signalized by the second battle of Pino de Agua on February 16-17, 1958. In the first battle, the rebels had been content to hit and run—after mauling the reinforcement column sent up from the plains. In this second battle they had determined to utterly wipe out the post and permanently deny it to the Batista forces. But when the rebels arrived there they found that word of their coming had preceded them—and the army had simply burned down the entire post and retreated down into the plains without even trying to fight! But since Castro's men were on the march, he decided to attack anyhow—against the heavy concentration of army forces at Estrada Palma, a nearby town.

There were one thousand regular army troops stationed in and around Estrada Palma. But so great was their terror of Castro and his men that they fled after offering only the feeblest resistance, leaving behind more than fifty dead, large quantities of automatic weapons and ammunition and three armored cars which had been wrecked by rebels hurling Molotov cocktails. So quickly and efficiently did the rebel bands withdraw after this attack that by the time Batista's air force arrived on the scene they were gone—and their bombs and bullets were expended on a deserted battleground.

It was shortly after this victory that the United States placed an embargo on all arms deliveries to the Batista government. This was a stunning blow to the Cuban dictator, not so much because of the arms ban itself (he could and did continue to receive arms from Britain, Trujillo's Dominican dictatorship and other sources) but because it signalized to Cubans the inevitable eventual downfall of the tyrant. Without American support Batista's days were clearly numbered. Even the most conservative Cubans would not wish to support a government whose principal ally (and the power which controlled so much of the Cuban economy) had deserted it.

Castro, sensing victory, called for a general strike throughout Cuba, to be combined with uprisings in the cities and a general offensive from the Sierra Maestra. This last was now possible largely because a landing strip had been cleared in rebel territory and on March 28 the first planeload of four tons of arms and ammunition had landed there from Mexico. But, basically, it was thought that the general strike would prove to be the heaviest blow, the one which would finally topple the Batista regime. It was set for April 9, 1958.

But a general strike, to be effective, demands complete political unity, the heaviest possible organization among the workers combined with their deepest understanding of the political content of the strike, and the protection of well-armed, well-trained and determined militants to ward off the blows of police and the army. None of these requirements was present on April 9. Political unity had not yet been achieved among the revolutionary groups. The Twenty-Sixth of July Movement was quarreling with the followers of Prío Socarrás in Miami; the Student Directorate had only loose connections to Castro's supporters; the Civic Resistance Movement which was ostensibly calling the strike was composed, for the most part, not of labor or rebel leaders but of middle-class merchants, college professors, professional men and manufacturers fed up with the Batista regime. And the Cuban Communist Party, which requested that its delegates be allowed to participate on the strike committees, was turned down cold. Indeed, a manifesto was put out by the Twenty-Sixth of July Movement denouncing Communist efforts to infiltrate the rebellion and warning people to beware of them.

As for organization among the workers and their understanding of the political aims and content of the strike, this too was lacking. To understand why, it is necessary to turn back momentarily to an examination of the sorry history of the Cuban labor movement. Once it had been dynamic: in the year (1933) which saw the overthrow

101

of the Machado dictatorship. In fact, it was largely because of the wave of strikes that paralyzed the Cuban economy in that year that Machado had been overthrown by the "Sergeants' Revolt" led by Batista. But when workers continued to strike against Batista-backed governments after Machado, the Cuban strong man had put them down ruthlessly. Nonetheless, the years of struggle had brought important benefits to those Cuban workers fortunate enough to belong to unions. Those years also saw a large-scale penetration of the Cuban labor movement by Communists. Cooperating with the new Batista regime, the Communists were able to advance to dominance in the labor movement during the 1930s. But after Batista left the country, during the Grau and Prío Socarrás governments, the Communists were driven from the labor unions.

In the years immediately preceding Castro's revolution, Cuban workers were organized into thirty-two industrial federations which were themselves part of the *Confederación de Trabajadores Cubanos* (CTC), claiming a total membership of more than one million workers. But the unions were bureaucratic, corrupt and little more than an arm of the government itself. CTC leaders supported Batista's takeover of power in 1952, declaring that the unions should "keep out of politics." Union members were consistently swindled of their dues, swindled of their votes in union elections, beaten and terrorized by union-hired thugs and gangsters and exploited by union-employer collusion. Any that showed a spirit of independence would be destroyed by Batista's order, and officials of the remaining unions (there were 1,641 local unions in Cuba) were personally, officially, and financially Batista's men. It was no wonder then that Cuba's working masses were effectively demoralized. It was premature, to say the least, to expect them to display deep understanding of the political motives and aims of the general strike of April 9, 1958.

And, finally—what of the well-armed, well-trained militants who would protect strikers and undertake acts of sabotage and the seizure of vital installations? Mostly these were to be students, led and organized by Twenty-Sixth of July underground workers and leaders. But they had almost no arms; they had no training to speak of; and, worst of all, such emphasis was placed on secrecy in preparing the

102

strike that they often had no chance to coordinate plans. A disaster was clearly in the making.

The Civic Resistance Movement issued the following proclamation:

1. The general strike will be declared at any moment. Everyone must be ready for it.
2. Lay in reserves of food and stocks of necessary items such as cooking oil, kerosene, candles and medicaments.
3. Immediately after you receive the order to strike, sabotage your place of work and leave with your workmates.
4. Stay away from work until the tyrant has fallen.
5. Keep away from any place where the forces of repression could find you.
6. Listen for the orders of the Twenty-Sixth of July Movement. . . .
7. Do not board any buses driven by police or strike-breakers. It could be extremely dangerous.
8. Owners of shops and offices which stay open will be regarded as collaborators with the dictator. It is therefore your duty to help close these establishments.
9. Employers who lay accusations against anyone who works for them or who informs on them will be dealt with as collaborators.
10. If a militant asks you for refuge, give it to him. It is the least you can do for a fighter for freedom.
11. Barricade the streets with dustbins, buckets, wood, vehicles, bottles, etc.
12. Make Molotov cocktails to throw at official cars. . . .
13. Pour oil and scatter nails over the streets.
14. Servicemen! If you are worthy of your uniform, do not fire on your brothers: desert and join their ranks. This is your chance to win their friendship.

Liberty or Death
26th July Movement

The general strike lasted just two hours. Everything went wrong. So tight had been the strike-leaders' security that many people did not even know the strike was supposed to take place that day. Trucks bearing Molotov cocktails never arrived, nor did automobiles full of pistols. The police had evidently been tipped off about many specific

José Miró Cardona

objectives and were waiting for the militants. The Communists not only did not support the strike—they actively sabotaged it, successfully defending Havana's CMQ-TV station against a group of students whose mission it was to seize it. Twenty-four hours after the "strike" failed, Batista's police had rounded up hundreds of suspects. About two hundred of them were shot; many were tortured to death. The underground movements in Havana and Santiago suffered a massive blow. And as soon as his forces had triumphed, the dictator issued claims that the entire strike had been organized by the Communists! This bald lie was intended to attract American support for his tottering regime, but the facts were too apparent to fool anybody.

And yet, behind Batista's victory on April 9, the dictator's power was crumbling. It was becoming more and more a hollow shell. His conservative supporters were fast becoming aware that the dictator

104

would no longer serve their purposes. His American allies had deserted him; the Catholic Church in Cuba formally asked that he resign to prevent further bloodshed; a group of Havana businessmen and lawyers submitted a petition to the same effect (for which their leader, José Miró Cardona, head of the Havana Bar Association, was driven into exile). As more and more Cubans became aware that their private distrust and hatred of Batista was shared by their fellow citizens, resistance against the tyranny became more widespread and public. And, above all, no temporary victory Batista might win over the disorganized workers and students of Havana could affect the course of the expanding war directed from the Sierra Maestra.

In only one month after the disaster of April 9, the rebel bands in the mountains of Oriente Province had increased their forces and strengthened their positions. The columns of Raúl Castro, Ché Guevara, Juan Almeida, Camilo Cienfuegos, Castro and others (there were soon to be eight columns in all) now numbered not scores or hundreds but thousands of men. Furthermore, they were being constantly supplied with tons of arms smuggled in from Miami and Mexico—sometimes by plane, sometimes by boat. And their communications with the plains and the cities were now very secure; new recruits, information and arms could reach them almost at will.

Raúl Castro's column was by now operating in the Sierra de Cristal; his men had already cut the telegraphic, rail and road communications in the valley that separated the Sierra de Cristal from the Sierra Maestra. In the month following the April 9 strike, Raúl's men captured a Batista document which showed that the United States, despite its embargo on arms to Batista, was delivering three hundred rockets to the dictator from the Guantánamo Naval Base on May 17. Enraged at what he considered American betrayal, Raúl had his men kidnap a number of United States Marines as well as a few American and Canadian civilians from the Guantánamo Base. But the United States had not, in fact, gone back on its embargo. What had happened was that a shipment of rockets made to Batista *before* the embargo had turned out to be faulty. The May 17 shipment was made only to replace them; since the embargo had gone into effect the U.S. government had made no new sales to Batista. When Fidel Castro learned of his brother's hasty action he immediately ordered the freeing of the captives. They were evacuated by American helicopters from the Guantánamo Base.

On June 29 Castro, with three hundred and fifty rebels, defeated more than one thousand Batista troops at Santo Domingo de Cuba. On July 20 a force of nearly two thousand regular army troops surrendered to Castro not far from Santo Domingo de Cuba—one factor in their defeat being the fact that the rebels had captured Batista's military codes. With the codes they were able to misdirect Batista's air force into bombing Batista's army units.

But the dictator still had more than thirty thousand troops in the field. And now, after many weeks of preparation, he loosed them in a great offensive against the rebel strongholds in Oriente Province. Tanks, armored cars, armored trains, bombers, fighter planes, artillery—everything was put into the struggle. Starting with light skirmishing on May 25, the Batista offensive continued until mid-August. But the fighting went against his forces. First of all, they were unfamiliar with the rugged terrain of Oriente Province. Secondly, they were surrounded by a hostile population who hastened to report their every movement to the rebels. Thirdly, there was no one to stand up and fight with. The rebel forces avoided open battles, disappearing into the jungles and mountains when outnumbered. They would only sally to the attack when they were sure of victory. Striking blindly and clumsily, like a maddened elephant trying to swat a fly, Batista's army saw its strength frittered away without results. Morale dropped steadily. By the end of the offensive, the army had suffered more than one thousand casualties and had lost six hundred weapons—including a tank, mortars, machine guns and automatic weapons of all kinds— to the rebels. Emboldened by this defensive victory, Castro decided the time had come to undertake offensive operations beyond Oriente Province.

His plan was relatively simple. Rebel forces would move down from the mountains to encircle and then capture Santiago de Cuba. Meanwhile the columns of Ché Guevara and Camilo Cienfuegos would march to the island's central province of Las Villas, where they would join forces to cut Cuba in two. Behind these military objectives there lay also a political objective. Under mounting pressure from all sectors of Cuban society, including the army, Batista had announced that elections would be held on November 3, 1958. He himself would not be a candidate, but he was supporting the candidacy of Dr. Andrés Rivero Agüero—and he was financing the opposition campaigns of several candidates, including former President Grau San Martín. It was very obvious that the entire election would be a fraud that would leave Batista still in control. Accordingly, Castro had ordered all Cubans to stay away from the polls on November 3. The expeditions of Cienfuegos and Guevara had as their secondary objective the enforcement of that order in central Cuba.

The march undertaken by Ché's and Cienfuegos' columns to reach Las Villas Province was an epic of endurance. Moving through territory not so friendly to their cause as Oriente Province, they were faced with lack of food, daily clashes against army units, daily air bombardment and night marches through swamps and over trackless mountains. But by October 6 Guevara and Cienfuegos had joined forces in the Sierra Escambray mountains in Las Villas Province.

The rebels arrived too late in Las Villas to really affect the election; they had to set up bases and lines of communications and establish themselves all during October. But the people of Las Villas spontaneously stayed away from the polls on November 3 in droves. The story was the same elsewhere in Cuba. In Havana 75% of the voters abstained; in the rest of Cuba even higher precentages refused to vote—in Oriente Province the figure reached 98%. The elections were a total failure and Batista had to remain his own front man.

December saw a steady advance by the rebels. Guevara captured Sancti Spiritus, Cienfuegos took Yaguajay, Raúl Castro took Sagua de Tánamo and Fidel himself closed in on Santiago. On December 29 the combined columns of Guevara and Cienfuegos took the large city of Santa Clara, capital of Las Villas Province (where they also captured one of Batista's armored trains). And almost everywhere in their path army garrisons were now surrendering without a fight. There were sharp little battles along their route of march, but it was clear that Batista's army no longer had any stomach for the battle.

This was evidenced directly on the night of December 28, 1958, when General Eulogio Cantilla, Batista's commandant of the Moncada Barracks in Santiago, arrived by helicopter to see Fidel Castro in the rebel camp outside Santiago. Cantillo brought a message from Batista declaring that the dictator was ready to resign provided the structure of the army was left intact and he personally was permitted to leave the country. Castro turned down both of these conditions instantly. He wanted Batista brought to trial for his crimes against the Cuban people—and he certainly did not intend to leave the old Batista army structure intact. Castro (as will be seen) had always had a deep distrust of the role played by the army, not only in Cuba but throughout Latin America. When these terms were rejected, Cantilla then offered to organize an uprising against Batista in Havana and pledged as a token of good faith that he would surrender the Moncada Barracks to Castro at 3:00 P.M. the following day without firing a shot. Although Castro well understood that Cantilla was hoping only to forestall the rebel takeover of state power, he agreed—it would perhaps save lives at Santiago. His suspicions of Cantilla's projected treachery were strengthened when Moncada Barracks did *not* surrender the following day, and confirmed when he received a message from Cantilla on December 30 that his proposed uprising against Batista would have to be postponed for a few days because of "unforeseen circumstances."

In any event, everything was over for Batista in Cuba. At 1:00 A.M. on January 1, 1959, the Cuban dictator released a message to the nation saying he was leaving the country in order to avoid further bloodshed. Then, with his family and a handful of his chief followers, he sped to a waiting aircraft at Camp Columbia (an army post outside Havana). At 2:10 A.M. the fugitives boarded a DC-4 and flew off into exile in Dictator Trujillo's Dominican Republic.

Behind him Batista left chaos.

General Cantilla desperately tried to put together a government of regular army officers and others tainted by connection to the fallen dictator's regime. But he failed within five hours. As dawn rose in Havana the General and his followers were placed under arrest by Twenty-Sixth of July Movement leaders in the capital.

When he heard the news of Batista's flight, Fidel Castro ordered a general advance on all fronts—and the immediate capture of Santiago. Cuba's second city fell to Castro's rebels on January 2, 1959, and Fidel himself delivered a speech to his followers and to the welcoming people of Santiago from that same spot in the Moncada Barracks where his men had been slaughtered five and one-half years before. By his side was Manuel Urrutia Lleo, the man whom Castro had already chosen to be the new president of Cuba, and Raúl Castro— and the spirits of hundreds, thousands of comrades who had fallen in the fight to make this moment possible: followers of the desperate attack on Moncada Barracks in 1953; those who had died on the long road from Mexico to Santiago; students, intellectuals, workers, underground leaders, and the many nameless *guajiros* who had lent him their strength and their hopes during dark days in the Sierra Maestra. There were many days of triumph ahead of Fidel Castro. He was to progress slowly over the eight hundred miles between Santiago and Havana, making speeches en route, being greeted by hundreds of thousands of his countrymen, making a triumphant entrance into Havana itself. But perhaps no moment in these victorious days was to match in intensity of feeling that moment when he took possession of Moncada Barracks—the scene of such complete defeat, and now of complete victory.

7

The Revolution Begins

This book is about a revolution. But a revolution is not simply a successful guerrilla war against a government, even though the existence of a successful guerrilla movement may be said to constitute proof that revolutionary conditions exist. Nor is it simply a successful rebellion that takes over a government: had the plotters of the Cienfuegos uprising succeeded, they would not have produced a revolution (indeed, they hoped to forestall one), but merely a violent transfer of the government's executive power. Classically, a revolution has been defined as a movement which succeeds in transferring political, social and economic power from the hands of one class within society to those of another. Thus the French Revolution transferred power from the hands of a decaying aristocracy into those of an upsurging middle class; the Russian Revolution intended the transfer of power from a decaying aristocracy and upper middle class to the workers and the peasant class. Likewise, if a revolution was to take place in Cuba, it would have to mean that real power—political, social and economic—had been transferred from the hands of the

upper-middle-class owners of factories, casinos, sugar mills, plantations, businesses and utilities and their military-political governing
apparatus into the hands of Cuba's workers and peasants (there
being no middle class sufficiently large and strong enough to take
power). It can be seen, then, that Fidel Castro's victory over Batista
was not in itself a Cuban revolution, but only the first necessary step
toward one; that is, *if* Fidel Castro and his Twenty-Sixth of July
Movement meant to carry out a real revolution, and not merely a
seizure of power.

But it was by no means clear that such was their intention. It
seems evident that at first neither Fidel Castro, Raúl Castro, Ché
Guevara nor any of their followers had any very dogmatic theory of
revolution. The impression one gains from Castro's "History Will
Absolve Me" speech is one of deep absorption in and study of Cuba's
problems. But his program of reform was pragmatic, not doctrinaire.
These young men were themselves scions of the middle class; the only
poverty and hardship they had ever known was that which they had
elected to suffer. Not that this was a necessary obstacle to their
carrying out a real revolution. Throughout history, most successful
revolutions have been led by such middle-class men as Danton, Lenin,
Trotsky, Sun Yat-sen and Mao Tse-tung. But unlike these revolutionary predecessors, the leaders of the Twenty-Sixth of July Movement were not theoreticians of revolution but practical men of action.
They knew, generally, the direction they wanted Cuba to take—
toward national independence of Yankee domination, toward political
freedom and social-economic development and justice. But how these
goals were to be reached was, at best, unclear.

Castro's attack on the Moncada Barracks in 1953 had been accompanied by a declaration stating that the rebel aim was to restore
the Constitution of 1940 which Batista had suspended. That constitution was, it will be recalled, an extremely liberal document. Had it
ever been truly enforced, it would have gone far to transform Cuban
society; for example, it banned large landholdings and called for severe
limitations on foreign landholding in Cuba. During his speech at his
trial, after the failure of the Moncada assault, Castro had declared
the aims of his movement to be: the restoration of the Constitution

of 1940; the assumption of governmental power by the revolutionary movement; the granting of ownership of the land to those who actually worked it; a profit-sharing plan in industry, and the confiscation of the property of top-ranking Batista supporters. This was a vague, liberal program, certainly not socialistic.

The years spent by the Twenty-Sixth of July men in the Sierra Maestra gave them some new perspectives on what Cuba needed. Living, working, fighting and suffering with the *guajiros* was a social and economic education for Castro and his followers. Castro had hoped to base his Movement on the support of the rural poor. He won that support and, hence, victory. He would not have been able to win *guajiro* support unless he had learned to formulate demands and programs that *guajiros* needed and wanted. First and primary among these was to gain ownership of the land—always the goal of any peasant class. Second was the establishment of civilization in the Cuban countryside: that is, of hospitals, schools, equality before enforceable law, etc. But all of this presupposed several things. It presupposed the confiscation of large landholdings, be they Cuban or foreign-owned; it presupposed the freeing of the Cuban economy from the burden of dependence on a single crop; it presupposed the ending of American domination of the Cuban economy both in agriculture and in industry; it presupposed the elimination of corruption and gangsterism from the Cuban government. And each of these aims was certain to arouse violent opposition—on the part of wealthy Cubans, American business interests, the American government and thousands of Cuban members of the governing apparatus, labor leaders, newspaper owners and other "establishment"-oriented people.

But during the early days of the anti-Batista struggle the Twenty-Sixth of July Movement needed all the supporters it could win. It was necessary to alienate as few people as possible. It was especially important not to alienate the United States government or the more influential American corporations which dominated the Cuban economy. The United States, which had intervened so often in Cuba's past might well intervene again to crush the revolt. These facts, combined with the fact that Castro and his followers were still "feeling their way" toward a revolutionary program, explain the shifting vagaries

113

of the manifestos and "statements of policy" that issued from the Sierra Maestra during the years of guerrilla warfare.

In November 1956 Castro had issued a manifesto which declared his aims to be "political sovereignty, economic independence, and a differentiated culture." It defined the Twenty-Sixth of July Movement as "democratic, nationalist and dedicated to social justice." No doubt to allay American fears, the manifesto also subscribed to "the Jeffersonian philosophy . . . and . . . to the formula of Lincoln of 'a government of the people, by the people, and for the people.' . . ." It spoke vaguely of "rectifying" foreign domination of the Cuban economy and "liberating" the country from the plantation system.

The first comprehensive political program announced by Fidel Castro after the guerrilla war began was the "Declaration of the Sierra Maestra" of July 12, 1957. This declaration set forth the policies of a provisional government which could expect Twenty-Sixth of July support (note that the Twenty-Sixth of July did not then, or ever, see *itself* as the future government of Cuba; it was only to be the armed support of such a government). These policies included the exclusion of any kind of foreign interference in Cuba's internal affairs; the exclusion of the military from Cuba's political life; the holding of general elections under the Constitution of 1940 at the end of one year after victory; immediate freedom for all political, civil and military prisoners; establishment of a civil service; free elections in all labor unions; redistribution of land to the landless; a campaign against illiteracy and for better and more widespread education; and an acceleration of the process of industrialization. Once again, a liberal, democratic program—revolutionary for Cuba, but hardly socialistic or communistic. It was upon this declaration that other groups fighting against Batista were able to agree and unite with the Twenty-Sixth of July Movement.

As victory in the guerrilla war approached, Fidel Castro (with the support, either grudging or enthusiastic, of the many splintered anti-Batista groups from Havana to Mexico to Miami) announced that Cuba's provision government would be headed by Dr. Manuel Urrutia Lleo, a justice of the Court of Appeal in Santiago, and José Miró Cardona, the well-known Havana lawyer who had been forced into exile by Batista. Urrutia was the single judge at the Moncada trial who had voted for the acquittal of Castro and his followers, on the grounds that since Batista had seized power illegally, armed revolt against his regime could not be considered illegal. Miró Cardona had been one of the signers of a petition demanding Batista's resignation during the latter days of the struggle. Urrutia was to be provisional president of Cuba, and Miró Cardona was to be prime minister. Neither man could be described as a revolutionary; both were anti-Communist to their cores. At most they were progressive liberals. Both men were installed in the Presidential Palace in Havana by January 2, 1959; immediately they started to organize a provisional government.

But even as Fidel Castro was making his slow, triumphant progress across Cuba from Santiago to Havana (speaking endlessly at every town, city and crossroads where people assembled to hear him), the first collisions between Cuban aspirations and Cuban realities were taking place. The United States government, which had shown little or no concern about the safety of American citizens under the lawless dictatorship of Batista, now demonstrated deep interest in the well-being of Americans in revolutionary Havana. This interest took the very concrete and threatening form of the appearance of three U.S. destroyers and two submarine tenders in Havana harbor, where they remained at anchor.

Now conditions in Havana after the downfall of Batista might certainly warrant the presence of United States warships to protect American citizens. Although no violence whatsoever had been offered to any American, the city was full of unruly mobs who were expending long-pent-up hatreds against the signs and symbols of the dictatorship. Everything that represented the Batista dictatorship in the public mind, from parking meters to gambling casinos, was being smashed. But in Cuban eyes, especially in the eyes of the victorious Twenty-Sixth of July men, this sudden appearance of American naval strength in Havana raised specters of past Yankee "gunboat diplomacy" and interference. These suspicions were strengthened by the emerging knowledge that the American ambassador, Mr. Earl T. Smith, in late December 1958, had been implicated in the maneuvers of General

Cantilla to seize power and forestall the revolution. But if the seeds of suspicion had thus been sown, they did not immediately bear fruit. Newspapers reported that the U.S. government was "optimistic" about the outcome of the Cuban revolution. And, on January 7, 1959, the United States officially recognized the new Cuban provisional government headed by Dr. Urrutia.

Without doubt the first events that sparked real Cuban-United States misunderstanding were the trials of former Batista leaders. The circumstances surrounding these trials aroused much popular revulsion in the United States and much popular resentment against that American revulsion in Cuba. But what were the real facts? After the flight of Batista and his top henchmen, the Cuban people demanded justice against those who remained. They were not crying for vengeance against politicians or soldiers *per se* simply because they had been associated with the old dictatorship; they were demanding justice against specific individuals accused of specific crimes. They were demanding justice against those professional gunmen who had shot down Cubans without trial; against those secret police agents who had tortured Cubans to death in Batista's prisons for years; against those army officers who had ordered the bombing of defenseless villages and the massacre of *guajiros* whose only crime was that they lived in the Sierra Maestra. Nor were the Cuban people demanding the blood of mere followers or executors of superior orders: they wanted payment in kind only from the men who gave those orders. The proof of this lies in the fact that from beginning to end of the trials, only about 450 individuals were executed. Had mass vengeance been exacted that number would have risen into the thousands. There is ample proof of the fact that it was the Cuban people and not the leaders of the Twenty-Sixth of July Movement who demanded this justice. Trials and executions took place all over Cuba in the early days of January 1959—in villages and towns which had not yet seen a single Twenty-Sixth of July rebel in the flesh. And the rebel radio, broadcasting from the Sierra Maestra, endlessly appealed to Cubans *not* to take vengeance into their own hands, to prevent bloodshed and not to stain the Revolution with mob violence.

Furthermore, the trials which were held throughout January 1959 were conducted according to the Cuban law under the provisions of the Constitution of 1940. But this in itself caused misunderstanding in the United States. For Cuban civil and criminal law was never based, as was American, upon the English Common Law. It was an outgrowth of Spanish law derived from Latin practice. Thus, for example, trials in Cuba were held without a jury of the defendant's peers, but before a panel of three judges (one of whom had to be a lawyer), two of whom had to agree to reach a verdict. The judges were empowered to decide what evidence was admissible or what witnesses should be heard. Defendants had the right to be represented by lawyers, to subpoena evidence and witnesses, and to appeal any verdict to a higher court within twenty-four hours after conviction. Did this system operate fairly in the trials of the *Batistianos*? That question would be impossible to answer in every case. But it should be noted that of 1,500 people tried for crimes committed under Batista's protection, *more than one thousand were acquitted* by the courts.

If it will be recalled that revolutions have never been gentle; that many thousands of American Tories faithful to the English Crown were mobbed, beaten, dispossessed (some killed) and driven into exile during the American Revolution without benefit of trial; that Madame Guillotine claimed literally thousands of victims during the French Revolution after only the flimsiest of trials; that the victims of the Russian Revolution numbered hundreds of thousands in its first years —then the revolutionary justice exacted in Cuba in 1959 would appear to be mild indeed.

Unfortunately, these historical facts were not remembered in the United States. Newspapers, eager for sensational stories, spread the impression that Cuba was running with the blood of the innocent, that maddened mobs were howling for the death of each and every defendant, that the trials were public spectacles like ancient Roman circuses in which Christians were tossed to the lions. And by January 16 angry protests against the trials were being heard in the United States Congress. Yet the fact remains that up to that time there had *not been one single* public-show trial held in Cuba; they had all been conducted in regular courts where the atmosphere was grave and decorous. It

117

was because of mounting American criticism of the trials that Castro decided to hold one in public so that all the world could see whether or not they were just. Accordingly, the trial of Major Jesús Sosa Blanco, one of the more notorious of Batista's henchmen, was ordered to be held in Havana's Central Park.

That this was a mistake was soon evident. Eighteen thousand Cubans attended the trial; more than forty-five witnesses testified that Sosa Blanco had burned their village and murdered their relatives. The crowd was unruly. It howled for the death penalty. And all of this was televised to the United States! Far from demonstrating to Americans that Cuban justice was just, it simply seemed to prove all the sensational charges in the American press. Of course Sosa Blanco was found guilty and condemned to death. But what was *not* televised to the United States, or widely reported in American newspapers, was the fact that he appealed the verdict and the Cuban Superior War Court *overturned it and granted him a new trial* because the public spectacle in Havana had not met judicial standards. At his second trial he was once again found guilty—and executed. As soon as Castro understood the American reaction to Sosa Blanco's trial he forbade any such "public" trials in the future, and in fact the trial of Major Sosa Blanco in Havana on January 22, 1959, was the *only* such trial held in Cuba at that time.

To further strain Cuban-American relations in the early weeks after Castro's victory was the problem of the *Batistiano* refugees in the United States. Many of these men were wanted as war criminals in Cuba, for such common crimes as torture and murder. Yet the U.S. government granted asylum to such men as Rolando Massferrer, former head of Batista's secret police, and others. The Cuban reaction to this was similar to what the American reaction might have been had Heinrich Himmler, former head of Hitler's infamous SS, been granted asylum after World War II in, say, Switzerland.

Yet by and large, the policy of the United States government toward Cuba in the days immediately after Batista's downfall was restrained. The administration of President Dwight D. Eisenhower was careful to disassociate itself from the more rabid attitudes expressed by some newspapers and some Congressmen. Ambassador

Earl T. Smith had been replaced on January 11 by Philip W. Bonsal, a man with no previous connections to the Batista regime. It was apparent that the American government was adopting an attitude of watchful waiting in regard to the new Cuban regime.

That regime reflected a peculiarity which has been noted of other revolutions. The actual Cuban government was composed of moderate liberals, men like Urrutia and Miró Cardona. Of seventeen cabinet ministers, only three had been with Castro in the Sierra Maestra. Yet this government depended entirely upon the continuing support of the Twenty-Sixth of July Movement and especially its leader. Real power, in other words, was in the hands of Castro and his followers, not in the hands of the Cuban government. This anomaly was observable in the American colonies just before the Revolution, when nominal power was vested in a Continental Congress but real power was held by such radical organizations as the Liberty Leagues and "Sons of Freedom" and Committees of Correspondence. It was observable in the French Revolution, whose National Assembly could not govern without the support of the Jacobin Clubs. It was especially notable during the Russian Revolution when a succession of post-tzarist governments found themselves unable to rule the country without the authority of the (then) unofficial Petrograd and Moscow Soviets to support them. But such governments have also, inevitably, come into conflict with the extralegal groups who hold real power. Historically, moderate middle-class governments have eventually refused to undertake the revolutionary programs demanded both by the situation and by the radical leaders whose power rests on the people's faith in them. Such a collision was also predictable in Cuba. When Castro and his followers demanded of the government reforms which went beyond what the government was prepared to give or to risk, the government, not Castro, had to give way. In fact, Miró Cardona resigned and was replaced by Castro as premier in February. Certain measures the Cuban government undertook immediately and in general agreement. It barred from holding public office all persons who had taken part in the 1958 elections; it dismissed thousands of Batista civil servants; it dissolved the old, corrupt Batista Congress; it legalized the Communist Party in Cuba. The Urrutia government also

119

announced that it would govern the country by decree for eighteen months, at the end of which time general elections would be held. United States response to these measures was generally favorable. No protests were registered.

Then came the reforms. Land and property which had been held by Batista's followers were declared to have been stolen from the Cuban people and were to be returned to them. Beginning in January 1959, redistribution of these lands was made to peasants throughout Cuba. The land was to belong to those who lived on it and worked it, but it could not be transferred by them except through inheritance. This measure was aimed at preventing penniless *guajiros* from selling their new lands to banks, mortgage companies or others who might then once again amass vast absentee-owned landholdings. Some two hundred thousand peasants benefitted from this early land redistribution program.

In March 1959 the price rates of the U.S.-owned Cuban Electric Company were cut in rural areas to match the price rates in Havana, and the U.S.-owned Cuban Telephone Company was put under government management (*not* ownership—the owners would continue to draw profits from their investment). Telephone service was expanded, especially in the countryside, and price rates were cut back to the 1957 level (they had been raised in 1957 at the insistence of the American ambassador). American response to these measures was, again, restrained. Ambassador Bonsal declared that the new government-imposed price rates were a matter between the suppliers and the users of telephone services—not a matter about which the U.S. government would concern itself.

It was in March also that several new governmental institutions appeared in Cuba. These were the National Institute of Savings and Housing, the National Tourist Agency and the National Institute of Agrarian Reform. The Savings and Housing Institute took over operation of the Cuban national lottery and devoted the money gained therefrom to the construction of new housing. At the same time a rent-control law was enacted which cut rents by 50% throughout Cuba and forced holders of vacant lots in the cities to either build on them or sell them to prospective buyers. This, plus an increase in

120

government-financed housing projects, began to eliminate land speculation and real-estate exploitation from Cuban life.

These early reforms were hard blows against those few wealthy Cubans whose prosperity depended on their real-estate investments. And in searching for some acceptable scapegoat for their discomfort, with unerring instinct they seized on the "Communist menace." It was they who first began to call Castro "Communist oriented," despite the many statements he had made of his opposition to the Communist philosophy. Not given to serious political reflection, the Cuban upper classes began to label the Twenty-Sixth of July Movement as a Communist conspiracy. This they did because of ignorance, a desire to inflame opinion in Cuba, and as a means of arousing American suspicions. It was partly to set these rumors and fears to rest that Fidel Castro visited the United States in April 1959.

Castro had announced that his visit would be unofficial. But he brought with him some of his top economic advisors. He met with Secretary of State Christian Herter and with Vice-President Richard M. Nixon. He did not ask for a loan, although the Cuban economy was in a perilous condition. Speaking before the National Press Club in Washington, Castro said: "We didn't come here to get money. Many men come here to sell their souls. We want only understanding and sympathy." In New York Castro declared: "We are against all kinds of dictatorships, whether of a man, or a country, or a class, or an oligarchy, or of the military. That is why we are against communism." He hoped for good relations with the United States. He said that Cuba would honor all the treaties signed by previous Cuban governments—including the one which had established the Guantánamo Naval Base. He said he welcomed private foreign investment in Cuba and that the new government would even give special tax exemptions to corporations which established themselves there. If Castro did not ask for American economic aid, neither was any offered by the U.S. government. Yet American officials might have understood that a man who had led a revolution which was to some extent anti-Yankee could hardly *ask* for Yankee dollars. But given the shaky state of the Cuban economy, Castro might gladly have accepted an American loan if it had been offered. Hindsight would

121

seem to indicate that the U.S. government missed an opportunity in April 1959 to show itself as the disinterested friend of a stable, peaceful Cuba.

If the early reforms of the Revolution had antagonized certain wealthy Cubans, the Agrarian Reform Law adopted on May 17, 1959, raised a howl of protest among them. The law stipulated that no individual could own more than 995 acres of land (except in certain cases where the limit was raised to about 3,300 acres)—nor could any corporation. Landholdings in excess of that would now be redistributed among Cuba's landless poor. Minimum allotments of sixty-six acres would be made to peasant families, and these would be organized into cooperatives so that they could pool machinery, labor and technical knowledge. The National Institute of Agrarian Reform would administer this program and was now empowered to supply seed, set prices, plan production and act as marketing agent. Subsequently, the Institute of Agrarian Reform was to snowball into a gigantic enterprise. But this was inevitable since it had assumed responsibility for financing production, directing the agricultural cooperatives, organizing rural training schools, supplying, maintaining and, finally, manufacturing farm machinery—and much else besides.

Although it was not yet clear how the new Agrarian Reform Law would affect American holdings in Cuba, U.S. reaction to it was swift. On June 11, 1959, the U.S. government delivered a formal note of protest to the Cuban government regarding the new land laws. The United States claimed it was not opposed to land reform, but that land *redistribution* might have an adverse effect technically on the Cuban economy. Furthermore, it asked what compensation the Cuban government was prepared to give to American individuals and corporations whose lands were seized.

To the technical criticisms of the U.S. protest, the Cuban government did not bother to reply. That, it was felt, was purely a Cuban internal affair. As to compensation, the Cubans announced that owners of expropriated lands would be paid in Cuban government bonds maturing in twenty years and paying 4½% interest—in Cuban currency, of course. As to what value would be set on the land, that would be based on the tax valuations which the owners themselves

122

had registered with the Batista government. This last was justice with a beautifully ironic twist. For American (and wealthy Cuban) individuals and corporations had been cheating Cuban governments for decades on their taxes. They had self-assessed their property at far below its real worth. Very well, suggested Castro; individuals and corporations could now reassess their property at its true worth. And, of course, pay taxes on the basis of this new assessment. In other words, landowning corporations and individuals were faced with the dilemma of either paying honest taxes on honest evaluation of their property or seeing it redistributed at very low rates of compensation.

Cuban landowners raised a storm of indignation over the Agrarian Reform Law. Once again they filled the air with accusations of Communist infiltration in the government. And their cries were soon reproduced by American businessmen who, either privately or through corporations, held heavy investments in Cuban land. Conservative Cuban newspapers printed front-page editorials denouncing the Castro regime—and some of these were reprinted word for translated word in the American press. The U.S. Congress now began to invite Cuban exiles to appear before various committees to testify to "Communist infiltration" of the Cuban government. Yet at that very time the Communist Party in Cuba had neither influence nor representation in the provisional government, and was bitterly opposed to many of its policies.

For causes which are still not entirely clear, on July 18, 1959, Fidel Castro resigned as premier, stating his reasons as being differences of opinion with President Urrutia. Of course this action, as Castro had foreseen, raised a wail of anguish throughout Cuba. In the upshot it was Urrutia who was forced to resign, while Castro returned as premier under the presidency of Osvaldo Dorticós Torrado—until then a minor government official noted only as one of the few Cubans who had publicly *opposed* the legalization of the Cuban Communist Party. Yet this fact did not prevent critics of the Castro government, both in Cuba and in the United States, from hinting darkly that Dorticós was a Communist and that Urrutia had been forced out because he was anti-Communist.

The resignation of President Urrutia was to mark a turning point in the continuing Cuban Revolution—and in U.S. attitudes toward it. By the time Urrutia had resigned and was replaced by Dorticós, Castro and his followers had learned some harsh facts about the difficulty of carrying through their cherished reforms in the face of intense opposition from Cuban and American corporations and their owners. Also, it seemed to them that their worst suspicions about American meddling in Cuban internal affairs were being proved correct. If further revolutionary progress was to be made, the Twenty-Sixth of July leaders would have to change tactics. On the other hand, the implementation of the Agrarian Reform Law coupled with Castro's rejection of the State Department's official note of protest regarding it had already significantly hardened official American opinion about the Castro regime. Both countries were now on a collision course. American policy toward Cuba was increasingly to be dictated by ignorance and greed; Cuban policy toward the United States was to be dicated by defiance and suspicion. Thus, only seven months after Batista's downfall, the seeds of impending disaster had been sown.

8

The Politics of Desperation

During the late summer of 1959 two new factors appeared to poison U.S.-Cuban relations. Each was real, and each was badly misinterpreted. The United States began accusing Castro and his followers of supporting armed invasions of other Latin American countries, and Cuba began accusing the United States of willfully allowing, if not actually encouraging and helping, single-plane sabotage raids over Cuban territory from Florida, carried out by Cuban exiles.

It was certainly true that both Fidel Castro and his closest supporters, Raúl (now head of the Cuban armed forces) and Ché Guevara, looked forward to revolutionary movements springing up all over South and Central America in the wake of their success. Ché was not the only non-Cuban who had followed Castro in the Sierra Maestra; there were others, many of whom hoped to repeat Castro's victory in their own homelands. And insofar as the Twenty-Sixth of July Movement had a viewpoint on the matter, it was definitely internationalist. It was hoped that the example of Cuba would encourage the peoples of Latin America to throw off the yoke of exploitive domination. And since that domination was in most cases carried on by very wealthy upper classes supporting reactionary governments allied with Yankee business interests, action against it could only take the form of revolutionary struggle with strong anti-American overtones. But the Cuban leaders realized (though perhaps not so profoundly as they ought to have) that anti-American rebellions in South America would be opposed by the United States not only because of Yankee commercial interests in the countries involved, but also, and perhaps primarily, because of American fears of upsetting the delicate world "balance of terror" between the United States and the Soviet Union. In that frightening balance which kept the Cold War from becoming a conflagration, continued American domination of the entire Western Hemisphere was an important weight. There were many American leaders who felt that the domination might well be replaced by a cooperative alliance, but their voices were seldom heard. And very few American politicians or military men could be found who would be willing to run any kind of risk with the basis of hemispheric defense. It was for this reason that the United States preferred to support governments (such as Trujillo's foul dictatorship in the Dominican Republic) totally repugnant to it rather than risk support of revolutionary elements who might introduce the dangerous element of *uncertainty* into U.S.-Latin American relations. American leaders (liberal as well as conservative), responsible, as they saw it, for the prevention of a war which might easily wipe out civilization or even the human race, tended to view Latin American revolutionary movements as direct assaults on the free world's security.

Castro and his followers may not have appreciated the American viewpoint in this matter, but they understood it well enough to realize that Cuban attempts to stir up rebellions in neighboring lands would meet instant and angry United States opposition. At the same time they understood only too well the craving of the broad masses of people throughout Latin America for a better, freer life. Nor did they suppose that a Latin America free of Yankee domination, whose people enjoyed some measure of social and economic progress, would pose any real threat to United States world interests. Castro had announced more than once that Cuban foreign policy would be "neutralist." He and his followers seemed to feel that an increase in the neutrality and power of the "third world" of unaligned nations would be a positive contribution to the defusing of the dangerous Soviet-American Cold War tensions. The examples of such nations as Yugoslavia and India were often paraded at this time by Cuban diplomats at the United Nations. Between United States fears and Latin American aspirations, Fidel Castro had his own "balance of terror" scales to adjust.

The results were not totally satisfactory. Revolutionary expeditions left Cuban soil several times during 1959 and 1960 intent on re-creating in other Latin American lands the same revolutionary program that had won victory in Cuba. Castro's government had a fair record of attempting to prevent such expeditions. On April 16, 1959, thirty-one Cubans were arrested outside Havana for plotting to organize an invasion of the Dominican Republic. On April 18, the Cuban army swooped down upon and dispersed a Nicaraguan rebel training camp in the province of Piñar del Rio. On April 28, a group of rebels succeeded in leaving Cuba bound for Panama, but the Cuban government claimed it had tried to prevent them (and later the Organization of American States completely exonerated Cuba from any complicity in the Panama affair). On May 6 it was reported that yet another Nicaraguan rebel group had been dispersed by the Cuban army. On August 3, still another band of six rebels preparing to invade the Dominican Republic was arrested by Cuban police. But it was hard for United States authorities to believe that Castro and his followers were not implicated in these attempts, even if they were put down by the Cuban government itself. And it was certainly true that such bands of rebels had Castro's sympathy. Nor, in view of his own beliefs and background, could he very well pose as the protector and defender of corrupt and reactionary Latin American governments. The truth was that with or without Castro's encouragement, the Cuban Revolution was bound to spark fires of rebellion throughout South and Central America—and that Cuba itself was bound to become a base for rebel expeditions. It might be recalled in this context that Castro himself had used nearby neutral Mexico as a base for his Twenty-Sixth of July Movement; and that the Mexican government had possessed sufficient knowledge of what was going on at Chalco and sufficient power to have absolutely squashed the rebellion, yet did not. The great majority of Latin Americans, including a number of Latin American political leaders, simply could not bring themselves to impose strict repression on other Latin Americans who sought freedom and justice through revolutionary means. Castro was one of these. His attempts to thwart rebel bands using Cuba as a base were halfhearted and, perhaps purposely, inefficient. The suspicion with which the United States government viewed Castro's regime was swiftly being replaced by alarm.

If the United States was increasingly worried about Cuban exportation of revolution, Cuba grew increasingly fearful of United States exportation of counterrevolution. The United States had provided refuge for many of Batista's top associates—and the Cuban revolutionary government well understood that these men would try any means to regain power. Fidel Castro and his followers recalled that most revolutions in history had sooner or later to fight against powerful counterrevolutionary attempts—usually carried out (as in the case of the French and Russian Revolutions) by exiles armed and supported by foreign nations. They were therefore extremely sensitive to the activities of former *Batistianos* (and post-Batista defectors) on American soil. When American Senators called for the admission of Batista himself as a refugee into the United States; when Congressmen and newspapers talked loosely of backing exiled Cubans who would restore "law and order" in their native land; when notorious Batista henchmen were respectfully heard by Congressional committees—Castro and his supporters saw evidence of a growing Yankee-backed conspiracy against them.

And in Cuban eyes the evidence took on more solid forms when single planes began to appear over Cuba dropping incendiary bombs into the sugarcane fields and counterrevolutionary leaflets on the towns. Several such raids were carried out during 1959 by planes based in the Dominican Republic—and in Florida. On October 21, 1959, Major Pedro Díaz Lanz, former chief of the Cuban air force (he was a regular army career officer who had continued to serve under Castro but resigned and fled to the United States when he was replaced by Juan Almeida), flew over Cuba dropping counterrevolutionary leaflets. Not long before, Major Lanz had testified to "Communist infiltration" of the Cuban revolutionary government before a Congressional committee.

The Lanz flight evoked an angry protest from Fidel Castro himself. He declared that he could not believe that the United States was so powerless that it could not prevent such flights from its territory. "I would ask myself," he said, "if the U.S. authorities would be so careless as to permit Russian emigrés to carry out bombing excursions over Russian cities and villages from Alaska. . . ." Castro voiced suspicions that the United States was even encouraging these flights. And when it is considered that some of the planes used were B-25 bombers which, although surplus and archaic, were certainly large enough to be noticeable, Cuban suspicions were understandable.

The American reaction to these Cuban charges was twofold. First, Ambassador Bonsal angrily denied U.S. complicity in them; secondly, Secretary of State Christian Herter as much as admitted that U.S. authorities had been guilty of negligence in trying to prevent them. He did this by issuing formal instructions to the Justice Department to take stricter precautions against such flights. One hundred additional immigration officers were dispatched to Florida to help enforce tighter control. But the truth was that it was all but impossible to absolutely control private flights from the *more than two hundred airfields* in Florida. Furthermore, as Bonsal pointed out, the United States government was not a dictatorship. The measures it could take to prevent supposedly peaceful domestic private flights from suddenly diverting to nearby Cuba were limited by law. Despite the fact that real efforts were made by American authorities to strictly enforce those laws, some flights evaded them. The raids continued although on a lessening scale. And Cuban suspicions began hardening into a certainty that the U.S. government was actively plotting the overthrow of the revolutionary regime.

An additional cause of mounting Cuban distrust of the United States was the fact that the American arms embargo instituted during the Batista dictatorship continued. When Castro sought to buy arms in the United States to fight back against the raiding planes he was denied them. And when he tried to buy fighter planes from England,

129

Dwight D. Eisenhower

the American State Department dispatched a note of protest to the British government, which then promptly cancelled the sale. The Americans were acting, as they thought, to prevent Cuban arming of revolutionary expeditions to other Latin American countries; Cubans were certain they were simply trying to keep the Revolution disarmed in order to make it easier prey for counterrevolutionary groups. The press and radio and TV in both countries were filled with angry charges and countercharges. And in the midst of this inflammatory situation, President Dwight D. Eisenhower, on October 28, 1959, stated that he was "puzzled" by the state of U.S.-Cuban relations. "On the basis of history," he declared, "one would have thought Cuba would be one of our real friends." The tragic lack of historical knowledge or perspective revealed by that remark was only a mild indication of the misdirection of American policy toward Cuba.

Despite these external tensions, the revolution in Cuba continued

130

to expand its social and economic effects. Under the Agrarian Reform Law, in October and November of 1959, the first American-owned lands were seized by the Cuban government for redistribution to landless peasants. These seizures were small-scale compared to the land areas seized from Cubans, and bonds were offered in compensation. (Both U.S. government and American corporation officials were to consider the proffered bonds as all but worthless, in spite of their interest rate, because they would be paid in Cuban currency.) In all, about 160,000 acres of American-owned land was seized at this time (as compared to the more than 2,000,000 acres already seized from Cuban owners). The properties included two large cattle ranches and mineral lands belonging to the Bethlehem Steel Corporation and the U.S.-owned Cuban Development Corporation. At the same time the Cuban government sealed the files of another forty American and Canadian corporations pending the enactment of a new petroleum law. Furthermore, oil companies were put on notice that they would either have to start developing their land (over half of all oil company land in Cuba was undeveloped) or lose their claims.

These last measures raised a storm of indignation among American businessmen. And that storm descended on the State Department, Congress and the administration of Dwight D. Eisenhower, as well as the press and TV. For the first time, bills were introduced in the House of Representatives calling on the United States to cut its sugar quota—that is, to drastically reduce the amount of sugar the United States bought from Cuba at a guaranteed price. American officials now, for the first time also, began saying openly what they had been hinting previously—that Fidel Castro and his followers were either secret Communists or under Communist Party domination. When it is recalled that the United States was just then emerging from the anti-Communist hysteria which produced such irrational phenomena as Senator Joseph R. McCarthy's accusations that the U.S. Army was "riddled with Communists," it will be seen that such charges, uttered by members of the government, were threatening indeed. And since much depends on whether or not these charges were true, or, if true, how they became true, it will be worthwhile to examine the history and position of the Cuban Communist Party.

131

The Communist Party in Cuba (calling itself the *Partido Socialista Popular*) was founded in 1925, during the days of the Machado dictatorship. It was, of course, forced to organize underground. Communists had been active in Cuban trade unions, especially the railway workers', tobacco workers' and weavers' unions. Its voice was powerful also in the National Confederation of Cuban Workers, a central labor organization. Actively opposed to Machado, the Communists took the lead in calling strikes and demonstrations against the dictator. Yet the Party did not support the final general strike which overthrew Machado, apparently because Party leaders feared that open insurrection on that scale would provoke armed American intervention. The general strike was successful in spite of the Communists, not because of them.

Despite the fact that the Grau San Martín government which succeeded Machado instituted widespread reforms and strongly opposed "Yankee imperialism," the Communist Party attacked it. Later Party apologists were to state quite frankly that Party leadership at that time was "confused." But it would not have had to be confused to oppose Grau San Martín, precisely because he *was* a reformer. From 1921 to 1937, the Communist Party around the world made all-out war on Socialist and other non-Communist leftist movements, calling them mere masks for the ruling classes and recognizing in their reformist programs a dangerous threat to that discontent among workers and peasants which is necessary to Communist success.

Once again, when the non-Communist left organized a general strike against the regime of Carlos Mendieta (a Batista front man) which succeeded the Grau government, the Communists abstained. When, in 1936, the world Communist line shifted momentarily in the direction of Popular Front cooperation with non-Communist parties, it was already too late to shake the strongly entrenched Batista regime in Cuba. And besides, by then the non-Communist left was very reluctant to cooperate with the *Partida Socialista Popular*.

Perhaps because of its divisive influence on the left, Batista legalized the Cuban Communist Party in 1938. At the same time he decreed a general amnesty for political prisoners and, under combined Communist-democratic pressure, issued the Constitution of 1940. We

132

have already seen that to Batista this was no more than a scrap of paper. But Communist leaders did not hesitate to say that "Batista found the path to democracy," and that he was even "the defender of democracy." The Cuban Communists actively campaigned for Batista during the 1940 elections, and themselves elected members to the Cuban Chamber of Deputies and to city councils throughout the island. Party leader Juan Marinello became minister without portfolio in the Batista government—thereby becoming the first Communist to join any government in the Western Hemisphere. When Batista resigned in 1944, the Communists continued to back his hand-picked candidate for the presidency, and when the Batista-Communist coalition lost to Grau San Martín, they found it possible to cooperate with the new president.

Cuban Communists defend their cooperation with Batista during his first reign on the grounds that he was then truly democratic and progressive. They claim that later he changed, and that the Twenty-Sixth of July Movement was too young to remember the older, progressive Batista, but only the later tyrant Batista. Such a defense of past Party policy was, of course, silly on the face of it. The truth was that Batista was an opportunist who would use any support, take any measures, whether "progressive" or "reactionary," to ensure his *personal* supremacy. Cuban Communists were simply too immature politically to recognize Batista for what he was: an opportunistic tryrant cut in the same pattern as many, many other Latin American "strong men."

In early 1947, the Grau government opened an attack on the Communists in Cuba's Labor Confederation. Communist strength among Cuban trade unions began to decline rapidly. By 1950 only a skeletal Communist group remained in the Labor Confederation. And in that year, Labor Confederation Secretary General Eusebio Mujal instituted a drive to ban Communists entirely from the Cuban labor movement. By 1957 Mujal was able to claim that no single Communist remained in any position of authority in any Cuban union. At the same time the Communists steadily lost popular support. They had registered 150,000 Party members in 1946, but by 1950 they could amass only 55,000 votes in the elections that year.

When Batista once again seized power in 1952, the Communists, after some hesitation, opposed him. Batista outlawed the Communist Party in 1953, and many Communist leaders went into exile, while others went to prison. Yet *some* Communists became part of the Batista government. It is still unclear why or how this could have occurred; the twisting and turning (one might say "squirming") of Communist Party methods and objectives in Cuba as in the rest of the world often defies reason. In Cuba, political opportunism probably combined with personal corruption to produce this strange situation.

The Cuban Communists, both those underground and those in the Batista government, hotly opposed Fidel Castro's attack on the Moncada Barracks in 1953, denouncing it as "adventuristic" and "bourgeois." As late as May 1958, the Cuban Communists were still denouncing Castro's guerrilla campaign as "irresponsible"—and they did their best to sabotage the general strike which failed on April 9, 1958. The Twenty-Sixth of July leaders responded by publicly asking why some Communist leaders were able to sleep comfortably in their beds in Havana while others carried on a bitter, armed struggle against the dictator. Castro and his followers consistently denounced the Communists and in many a personal interview expressed their disgust with and hostility to the Party's wavering policies and leadership.

After Castro's victory he continued in the press, in public speeches, on radio and TV to attack Communists and communism generally. Times without number, Castro and other Twenty-Sixth of July leaders announced that theirs was a "humanist" revolution and against dictatorship by the left as much as dictatorship by the right. In May 1959, Twenty-Sixth of July candidates, organized in a "labor humanist front" under the leadership of David Salvador, defeated Communist candidates in trade-union elections throughout Cuba. The defeated Communists unleashed bitter attacks on Castro and his followers in their newspaper *Hoy* (*Today*), and feeling against them was so strong that police had to be detailed to guard the *Hoy* offices in Havana. Castro's anti-communism had been consistently reported in the American press by responsible journalists, and it was affirmed by the United States Central Intelligence Agency, whose deputy director,

General C. P. Cabell, testified before a Senate Committee in November 1959: "We believe that Castro is not a member of the Communist Party, and does not consider himself to be a Communist." Furthermore, Cabell reported, "Within the Twenty-Sixth of July Movement there is considerable evidence of opposition to communism."

But if Castro and his followers were anti-Communist they were also determined on two things. First, they would not attack the Communists in such a way as to endanger the Revolution itself. Since Castro's victory, the Cuban Communist Party had supported most of his reforms (though they opposed others). To join with reactionary Cubans in an orgy of anti-Communist activity would be to support counterrevolutionary interests. Secondly, Fidel Castro and his supporters were not about to go around proclaiming themselves anti-Communist simply to reassure nervous American officials or businessmen, who were in any case opposed to the Revolution. Cubans were all too sensitive to the humiliations they had suffered from American intervention in the past. They refused to act before the Cuban people as if they were obediently catering to American fears and pressures.

None of all this was of any avail. Many American businessmen and many officials in the American government were determined that Castro and his followers were Communists or Communist dominated. When, at a general meeting in November 1959, the Cuban Labor Confederation repudiated Communist delegates and, again under David Salvador's leadership, forced Communist trade-union candidates to withdraw from the convention, American response was to cry that this only proved Communist domination of the Cuban labor movement and that David Salvador himself must be a Communist! (This last charge, based on the fact that once, many years before, Salvador had worked as a proofreader on an obscure Communist Havana newspaper, became even more ironic in 1961 when Salvador was imprisoned—for being anti-Communist!) One thing became very clear to Castro and his chief lieutenants: Whether they were Communists or not, the United States would denounce them as such. Why? It could only be, they thought, part of a program to set Cuba up for some counterrevolutionary attempt. Furthermore, as they realized that many

Americans were willing to lie baldly about affairs in Cuba, they began to wonder if those same Americans had not been lying all these years about conditions in the Soviet Union. They knew they themselves were not Communists, and they knew they intended no "menace" to democracy or the "free world." Perhaps, then, all those American warnings of the peril of international communism were just as unfounded as their warnings about the perils of the Cuban revolution.

As has been pointed out before, the personal backgrounds of Fidel Castro, Raúl, Ché Guevara and other Twenty-Sixth of July leaders were essentially middleclass. Of all of them perhaps only Ché had studied Marxism in any serious way. The day-to-day necessities of the Revolution could well combine with American denunciations to start them on the road to deeper sympathy and closer cooperation with Communists, especially when it is recalled that none of the Twenty-Sixth of July leaders were dogmatists. They might well be attracted to a party and a movement based on more than one hundred years of intricate theorizing, a party and movement furthermore that seemed to support the most essential parts of their reform program. But even all these circumstances and pressures would not have been sufficient to throw the Twenty-Sixth of July Movement into the embrace of the Communist Party. Only overt actions could accomplish that. Unfortunately the actions were not long in coming.

As has been pointed out, Cuba's was a one-crop economy. The island's prosperity, in fact its very economic life, depended on the production and sale of sugar. Fully 80% to 90% of all Cuban exports were sugar sales to the United States and the rest of the world. During the Great Depression in the United States, when domestic beet and cane sugar growers complained that they could not compete with Cuban sugar sales, Congress, through the Jones-Costigan Act of 1934, restricted the amount of sugar imported from Cuba to about 30% of U.S. internal consumption. But, for this 30%, the United States agreed to pay a fixed price per ton which was generally (but not always) much higher than the world price. In this way American domestic sugar producers were protected; the U.S. was assured of a continuing supply of Cuban sugar, and Cubans were assured of a fairly fixed income. In fact, after that, Cuban governments made a practice of fixing limits on Cuban sugar production so as to avoid overfulfilling their domestic, U.S. and world market possibilities. In 1948, following a decline in world sugar prices, the United States adopted a new Sugar Act which guaranteed the purchase of about half of Cuba's sugar production—at prices substantially higher than those prevailing elsewhere. It need not be pointed out that though this was of important benefit to the Cuban economy, much of this American-guaranteed price was paid to American, not Cuban, corporations which controlled the Cuban sugar industry. When American government officials, Senators and Congressmen began to talk about cutting Cuba's sugar quota, they were talking about dealing the Cuban economy a ruinous blow—declaring economic war, in fact. And in January 1960 it was revealed that the Eisenhower administration had decided to ask Congress for authority to manipulate sugar quotas.

It was into this tense situation, in February 1960, that Anastas I. Mikoyan, First Deputy Soviet Premier, and his traveling Russian Trade Fair walked. The visit of the Russian Trade Fair had been planned long before. It had already visited the United States and Mexico. But to Cuba it represented an opportunity out of an economic impasse. At the opening of 1960, Cuba found herself with a sugar surplus of about one and a quarter million tons—the largest in nine years. At the same time the world price for sugar had fallen to its lowest level in eighteen years. When the Soviet Union declared that it would be willing to buy Cuban sugar over a long-term period at a fixed price, it seemed a golden opportunity to the Castro government. Not only had Cuba no hope of expanding its U.S. market, but that market was now threatened with foreclosure. Accordingly, on February 13, 1960, Anastas Mikoyan and Fidel Castro signed an agreement whereby the Soviet Union agreed to buy five million tons of Cuban sugar over a five-year period at approximately the world price. The Russians agreed to pay 20% of the price in dollars, the rest in manufactured items, crude oil, etc. This was not so good a bargain as Castro might have struck with the United States. Indeed, he had offered to sell as much sugar to the United States as it could consume, but his offer had been ignored. The Russian price was lower than the U.S. quota price, and only a small part of it would be paid in

137

Anastas I. Mikoyan

the hard currency that Cuba desperately needed to buy manufactured goods. On the other hand, Russian manufactured goods would be welcome. The agreement added a stabilizing factor to the Cuban economy. Besides, the United States was not about to buy more Cuban sugar—it was about to buy less.

Cuba had sold sugar to the Soviet Union for years. Shipments amounted to more than 1,100,000 tons during the last four years of the Batista regime. But American critics spoke as if there had never before been any kind of trade between Cuba and Russia; as if other South American countries, notably Brazil, had not been trading profitably with the Soviets for years. The Cuban-Russian trade agreement was paraded as positive proof that Castro's government was now enslaved by Moscow. And when a short time later Cuba and Russia opened formal diplomatic relations with an exchange of ambassadors, some Americans spoke of "Soviet penetration" of the Western Hemisphere as if Russia had not maintained diplomatic relations with Mexico, Argentina and Uruguay for many years.

Yet American fears were not completely unjustified. For Cuba's was a revolutionary government, undertaking a revolutionary social and economic transformation of the nation's life. This revolution was being presided over by men who were essentially pragmatists, who had few domestic economic resources and very little experience in economic affairs, and felt themselves to be under mounting foreign pressure. It was more than likely that their trade agreement with the Soviet Union would in fact result in very much increased Soviet penetration of Latin America by way of Cuba and increased prestige for the Cuban domestic Communist Party. But it is very hard to see what alternatives the U.S. government left to Castro.

Castro's suspicions of American intentions reached the boiling point on March 4, 1960, when the French munitions ship *La Coubre* exploded in Havana harbor with a roar that could be heard for miles. Seventy-five people were killed and more than three hundred injured. Castro charged that the ship had been blown up by American sabotage. The United States, he pointed out, had prevented the Cuban government from buying arms from any country that would bow to American pressure. At the same time, the United States had been strangely unable to control bombing flights over Cuba carried out from Florida bases. And now the U.S. government was about to cut the Cuban sugar quota. Was it not reasonable, the Cuban premier demanded, to at least *suspect* American involvement in the *La Coubre* explosion? No, replied the State Department, it was not—and such charges amounted to an atrocious slander against the United States government. It was reported unofficially that President Dwight D. Eisenhower was personally enraged over Castro's charges.

In all of this one may detect a melancholy resemblance to things past. The United States was no more guilty of blowing up the *La Coubre* than Spain was of blowing up the *Maine*. But Fidel Castro and the Cuban people were as firmly convinced that somehow the United States was basically responsible as William McKinley and the American people had been that Spain was responsible in 1898. The

139

La Coubre probably blew up without anyone's assistance, as, probably, did the *Maine*. If anyone had been guilty of sabotage the odds are overwhelming that it would have been former *Batistianos* precisely attempting to involve Cuba and the United States in hostilities (as the *colons* of old tried to involve the United States and Spain). And if Spain had tolerated *colon* activities, the United States was certainly tolerating Cuban counterrevolutionary activities, as the bombing flights from Flordia demonstrated. Nonetheless, after he had cooled off somewhat, Castro formally retracted his charges and the Cuban government made a public apology to the United States for having voiced such suspicions.

But the continuing public "dialogue" between Cuba and the United States became only a mask for American plans after March 17, 1960. For on that date, barely two weeks after the *La Coubre* explosion, President Dwight D. Eisenhower secretly directed the Central Intelligence Agency to begin to enlist, train and equip a Cuban counterrevolutionary force to invade the island at a propitious moment. The United States government thereby undertook to sponsor the armed overthrow of an independent non-Communist neighboring government. American charges, reactions and policy toward Cuba from that time on must be viewed in that light.

And what of the accomplishments of the government that the United States now planned to overthrow? By March 1960 the Cuban revolutionary government had built 270 new rural schools and 45 new or expanded hospitals. It built hundreds of miles of new roads and constructed many new bridges. It had raised the enrollment in childrens' nurseries by 50% and granted more than $75,000 in school scholarships to poor children (as compared with $5,000 in 1958, the last year of the Batista regime). It had turned over control of the labor unions to men honestly elected by union members (Communists, it will be remembered, were excluded). It had opened more than 450 "peoples' stores" on taken-over land, where *guajiros* bought things at near-cost prices. It had distributed millions of acres of land to the landless. The government Tourist Agency had opened up miles and miles of Cuba's beautiful beaches to the Cuban people themselves. Hotels, casinos and resorts that had been the high-priced domains of

140

the wealthy or of rich American tourists were now available for en-
joyment by the people of Cuba. Independent surveys made by American individuals and groups in the spring of 1960 reported that more
than 80% of the Cuban people supported their government enthusi-
astically and were especially devoted to Fidel Castro. This was the
government that the United States was now secretly preparing to
destroy.

President Eisenhower's decision on March 17, which was at first
known to only a handful of men in the Central Intelligence Agency
and the Pentagon, was soon to become one of the worst-kept "secrets"
in American history. The deterioration of Cuban-American relations
progressed with increasing momentum into an abyss of bitterness.
Charges and countercharges, actions and reactions multiplied.

In April 1960, President Eisenhower and Cuban President Dorticós
both sent open letters to a meeting of the Chilean University Students
Federation. Each accused the other's government of endangering
hemispheric peace. In May, for the first time, Castro accused the
United States of planning to invade Cuba with a mercenary army of
Cuban exiles—a charge which was ridiculed by the American State
Department. In that same month Castro notified U.S.-owned oil
refineries in Cuba that they would be required to process crude oil
shipments due to arrive from the Soviet Union as part of the Russo-
Cuban Trade Agreement. A few days later the State Department
announced it was ending all technical aid to Cuba and that the nine
American technicians there would be withdrawn. In June, the U.S.
government again denounced Castro for his "slanderous" charges that
the United States was preparing to intervene militarily in Cuba. More
importantly, the U.S.-owned oil refineries in Cuba refused to process
Soviet oil—and were promptly seized by the Cuban government.

Action—and reaction. Seizure of the U.S. oil refineries was followed, on July 6, 1960, by the long expected cut in Cuba's sugar
quota. In turn, the Cuban government adopted a law permitting the
seizure of any and all foreign-owned businesses in Cuba whenever
necessary. And the seizures began, first the two largest U.S.-owned
sugar mills, then U.S.-owned rubber companies. Meantime, a Presidential election campaign was under way in the United States. Demo-

141

cratic candidate John F. Kennedy accused Eisenhower-supported Republican Richard Nixon of being unable to cope with the "Communist menace" in nearby Cuba. He charged that the Eisenhower administration had been "soft" on the Cuban Revolution. Perhaps to counter this charge, the Eisenhower administration revealed that a complete embargo on goods to Cuba was being planned. On October 19 the embargo was imposed: only medical supplies and foodstuffs were henceforth permitted to be exported to Cuba. Castro immediately sent Ché Guevara to Eastern Europe where he signed trade agreements with several Soviet-bloc countries. He also signed another agreement with the Soviet Union under which the Russians promised to build more than one hundred factories in Cuba and send over the necessary technical and supervisory personnel to teach Cubans how to run them. Then, on January 3, 1961, President Eisenhower, declaring that there was a "limit to what the United States in self-respect will endure," broke off all diplomatic relations with Cuba.

This was Eisenhower's last official "contribution" to Cuban-American relations. On January 20 the United States had a new President, John F. Kennedy. But not a new Cuban policy. When Fidel Castro publicly expressed the hope that the new administration would undertake a revision of U.S. policy toward Cuba and "begin anew" in an attempt to recreate friendly relations, the new President declared that he had no intention of reestablishing relations with Cuba at that time.

From the viewpoint of some Americans, especially those involved in the secret invasion planning, the stage had now been set. The Castro government had been publicly painted as "Communist dominated." The Cuban economy had been dealt severe blows and Cuba had been diplomatically isolated in Latin America. Castro had been forced into expropriation of U.S.-owned businesses. His constant charges that the U.S. was plotting aggression only further inflamed American public opinion against him.

And the stage had been set in Cuba, too. By early 1961 Fidel Castro and his leading supporters had come to rely more and more on Communists as their chief lieutenants in carrying out radical reform measures. It seemed that only Cuban Communists could be relied on to support the revolutionary government at all costs. And among govern-

142

ments, only the Soviet Union and other Communist nations such as Poland, Hungary and Red China, with each of whom trade agreements had been signed, encouraged Cuba to carry forward programs that most Cubans endorsed. As Communist influence in the Cuban government increased, some of Fidel Castro's early supporters began to desert him. These were men like Manuel Ray, Raul Chibás and Felipe Pázos, all strong Twenty-Sixth of July men. Like Castro himself in the early days, these Cubans did not intend to see Soviet imperialism replace Yankee imperialism in Cuba, nor did they intend to replace the Batista dictatorship by a Communist Party dictatorship. They felt that Castro's increasing reliance on and cooperation with the Communists was a betrayal of the Revolution. When David Salvador, the Cuban trade-union leader who had effectively barred Communist penetration of the labor unions (and had been denounced in the U.S. as a Communist for his efforts), was arrested on charges of "treason" while trying to escape from Cuba in a small sailing boat, it seemed to many impartial observers that Castro had indeed elected to follow the Communist road. But what no one was able to point out was any other road he could have followed to preserve his revolution in the face of American opposition.

And meantime, during the early months of 1961, the Cuban government, at the United Nations and elsewhere, continued to accuse the United States of planning an invasion with the purpose of overthrowing the government. At the United Nations and elsewhere, the United States government continued to indignantly reject such accusations.

9

The Politics of Ignorance

When President Dwight D. Eisenhower, on that fateful March 17, 1960, secretly ordered preparations to begin for an eventual invasion of Cuba by Cuban exiles armed and trained by the United States, he was acting, as any American President must act, on the basis of advice and information supplied to him by such agencies as the State Department, the Central Intelligence Agency, and the Defense Department. The information he received was wrong, the advice bad. None of it, however, was malicious at the level it was given or received. That is to say, none of the President's top advisors was particularly bloodthirsty or warlike. As for the President himself, few men knew war better or detested it more than the former Allied Supreme Commander in Europe during World War II. If Eisenhower and his chief aides felt that only violence could solve the "Cuba problem," it was not because they welcomed violence, but because they were sincerely convinced that the application of force against the Castro government in its early years would avoid the necessity of much greater violence later. All of which, of course, presupposed a particular view of what that government and its leaders were. This view was so disastrously mistaken that it deserves examination.

Among the many things that an American President must be (Chief Magistrate, Commander-in-Chief of the Armed Forces, Chief Executive and, in a very real sense, Chief Legislator), he is not required to be a historian. The historical view of Cuban-American relations revealed by the Eisenhower decision was, in brief: We had always befriended Cuba, had poured heavy investments into the island, had protected it against possible outside aggression, had won for it its freedom from Spain, had generally been a force of stability in the island's affairs, and had used our great strength moderately in Cuba from time to time—only for the island's own good. Whether this historical view was correct may be judged from the history recounted in these pages. Correct or not, it was certainly not, nor had it ever been, the Cuban view of Cuban-American relations.

Nevertheless, if the above historical perspective is assumed, then the touchiness, the pride and the hostility of Castro's Cuba toward the United States would seem inexplicable—unless it was the result of a plot. And if it was the result of a plot, then that could only be a Communist plot and must involve Communist forces beyond Cuba as well. And if that was true, then the Cuban revolution was itself simply a forerunner of Communist penetration of the Caribbean and Latin America. And such a penetration would pose threats to United States security which were unacceptable in an atomic age. Furthermore, President James Monroe's celebrated Doctrine, one of the foundation stones of American foreign policy for more than a century, would appear to be threatened: Cuba would certainly become, in fact if not in name, a Soviet colony in the New World.

There runs through the statements and writings of President Eisenhower about Cuba a thread of real and sincere puzzlement over the deterioration of Cuban-American relations after the Castro victory. That puzzlement finally was resolved by the acceptance of the Communist-plot theory. And based both on the President's historical knowledge and the daily information he received from advisors, such a theory did not seem to him implausible. At a later date that theory would be not only plausible but true. But at the time of the President's decision it was false. And it was to remain false for more than a year. Fidel Castro was not then a Communist, nor was Cuba a Communist dictatorship, nor was Cuba anxious for any but the best relations with the United States. On several occasions during 1960, both Castro and Cuban President Dorticós appealed for a new beginning in Cuban-American relations, an adjustment of differences. These appeals, like the offer of Brazil to mediate between the two nations, were turned down by the United States.

Why did officials close to the President assure him that Cuba was following the path to communism and would soon be a Communist puppet state? That Fidel Castro and other Cuban leaders were either secret Communists or Communist dupes? This misinformation was supplied, again, not maliciously, but out of profound ignorance.

The State Department is a huge organization. Like all huge organizations it tends to be cautious, conservative and unimaginative. Every American President since Franklin D. Roosevelt has had occasion to complain (sometimes bitterly) about the State Department's ponderous ways, the obstructionism it displays against policies of which it disapproves, the timidity with which it bows before outside pressure groups. Under "strong" Presidents, such as Roosevelt, Kennedy and Johnson, the Department has often been bypassed or simply ignored in foreign policy matters. But Eisenhower was very much a "teamwork" President who relied more than some on the advice and suggestions of his assistants. Yet in its basic views of the Cuban Revolution, the State Department reflected the views of many Americans, and should not for that reason be singled out for special criticism.

To many, perhaps most, Americans, certainly most Americans in a position to influence the State Department, the American experience of freedom is the only one conceivable. That freedom has been firmly rooted in the private ownership of the means of production—capitalism. And the American system of free enterprise has produced not only freedom, but a remarkably high standard of living for most Americans. Furthermore, it has been based upon, and in turn has developed, a pattern of personal self-reliance and independence among the American people. This simplistic view overlooks several basic facts: e.g., that American personal liberties are based on cen-

147

turies of development of the British Common Law and, like English personal liberties, are all but unique in the world anywhere; that American wealth has been the result much more of the fortuitous and brutal exploitation of a vast virgin continent than of the system under which that exploitation was carried out; and that the picture of the "self-reliant" and "independent" individual American has been, with some notable exceptions, largely a historical myth. None of these affected Americans' self-views or, hence, their views of what was happening in Cuba.

To most Americans, government seizure of private property, even with compensation, is a direct attack on personal freedom. Thus when Cuba's Agrarian Reform Law first went into effect, some Americans protested the seizure of land from giant corporations; but since that land was to be redistributed to small private owners, the weight of American private opinion supported the move. In this case government seizure, though lamentable, was after all aimed at furthering, not restricting, private enterprise. But when the newly distributed lands were organized into cooperatives, American officialdom began to worry; when it became clear that these cooperatives would be state-run and state-administered, Americans looked upon them as but one step away from collective farms and a means of stamping out personal liberty and independence. That was why American notes to the Cuban government constantly reiterated the fact that the United States was not opposed to land reform—only to the way Cuban land reform was being carried out.

Most Americans set great store by democratic forms: elections, assemblies, voting rights, the Constitution, etc. When these or similar forms are not observed in foreign countries, Americans tend to assume that the people of those countries lack freedom, that their governments are tyrannies. In most cases they are right. But they tend to overlook the fact that observance of the forms of democracy does not always guarantee freedom. Batista maintained most of the outward trappings of democracy: a "free" parliament (bribed and intimidated to the point of uselessness); a "free" judicial system (also mostly corrupt and terrorized); "free" elections (in which voting frauds and violence predicted victory); "free" enterprise (free to pay bribes instead of taxes); "free" unions (run by gangsters), and a "free" press (most newspapers being subsidized by the Batista regime). Despite the fact that Americans knew very well that Batista was a dictator, and a particularly violent one at that, these outward shows of "freedom" were sufficiently satisfying to prevent the U.S. government from attacking the Batista regime. That regime was hated by the overwhelming majority of Cubans. But because, in the years immediately following Castro's take-over, the promised elections were not held, although all the other above-listed freedoms were truly observed, Americans assumed that the revolutionary government must be a dictatorship. To a certain extent they were right. But more than 80% of all Cubans heartily supported Castro and his reforms. It was a dictatorship of the popular will, not a tyranny.

Given all this, it was incomprehensible to most Americans, and to their government, that Cuba's workers and peasants cared less about the freedom of "free enterprise" than about seeing their children fed, clothed and schooled, seeing themselves housed decently, organized into honest unions and paid a living wage, seeing their country develop its own resources free from foreign domination. It was only among precisely those groups of Americans (especially black Americans) who had themselves suffered the kind of deprivation to which Cubans had long been accustomed that any sympathy could be found for Fidel Castro and his government. But these Americans—those who were the uninvited guests at the American banquet of prosperity —had but little influence at the State Department.

Those who did have some influence there, and who made it their business to use that influence in regard to the Department's views of the Cuban situation, were the corporate and business interests who stood to lose their investments in the Cuban economy. Representatives of American sugar mills, oil companies, mining, utility companies, ranching companies and many other enterprises in Cuba bombarded not only the State Department, but perhaps more importantly, their Congressmen and Senators with protests, warnings and misinformation about Cuban affairs. That the long-run interests of the United States might not coincide with their private interest in maintaining a steady flow of profits for their stockholders never

149

seemed to have occurred to these corporations. Nor did it, apparently, occur to the American government. These were, after all, the years during which an American Secretary of Defense could state: "What's good for General Motors is good for the country."

These were some of the complex factors that led President Eisenhower to decide on armed intervention in Cuba as early as March 17, 1960. Once that decision was made, its carrying out was turned over to the Central Intelligence Agency and the Pentagon. But there were certain restrictions imposed upon these "experts." One of them was that the United States must not appear to have taken any direct part in the invasion. It must be explainable as simply an effort, not unlike Castro's own, by exiled Cubans, anxious for their country's welfare, to overthrow a tyrant. This was meant to reassure other Latin American nations long sensitive to Yankee imperialism in the Western Hemisphere, and to provide a face-saving device before world public opinion. Because of this precondition, the actual planning and arming and training of the invasion would be left in the hands of the C.I.A. The Pentagon would act only in an advisory capacity. After all, the C.I.A. had been successful in overthrowing one Central American government recently, that of Guatemala—why not another? The viewpoint of the American government, and especially of those charged with organizing and preparing the invasion, could only be characterized as the "comic-book" view of history, politics and foreign affairs—if that viewpoint had not had such tragic results.

Basically, the "comic-book" attitude toward history and world politics (to which the C.I.A. and the Pentagon have long adhered) may be stated as the belief that: (1) morality in world affairs is what best suits American interests; (2) in any case, morality in world affairs is a myth—and an unimportant myth at that; (3) the application of sufficient force, whether that force be military or monetary, is capable of solving moral problems; (4) there are military solutions to political problems; (5) given sufficient financial and coercive means, masses of people are capable of being manipulated in any chosen direction; (6) individuals "make" history as they choose: the daring of a secret agent, the cunning of a spy, the bravery of

150

soldiers—all these may stem or change broad historical movements in the affairs of men. The disasters this attitude has provoked, not only in Cuba, where it led to support for the Batista regime, but also in such places as China and Vietnam, do not seem to have undermined its cherished place in military thinking. It is not uniquely American. The Soviet interventions in Hungary and Czechoslovakia and elsewhere are based upon the same attitudes and will eventually produce the same results.

Given this outlook on the part of those who planned the invasion, all else was bound to follow. It was assumed that a revolution could simply be "created" and that a guerrilla war based on that "revolution" could be maintained. But guerrilla wars depend almost entirely on the real cooperation and support of the broad masses of the people. That has been proved time and again—in Spain in 1812, in Yugoslavia during World War II, in China from 1930 to 1949, and in Cuba itself from 1956 to 1959. It does not matter how well trained, well equipped or well led the guerrillas may be—they must have the support of the people; they are the armed expression of the popular will, basically political instruments, not military. How little this has been understood by the American military is demonstrated by the U.S. Army's training of soldiers in "guerrilla warfare" as if it consisted solely or even primarily in learning how to creep silently through jungles or survive on a diet of roots and insects.

During the spring and early summer of 1960, C.I.A. agents recruited exiled Cubans living in Florida and elsewhere to join an invasion force which would overthrow the Castro regime. At the same time work was started on the construction of a highly secret training and supply base at Retalhuleau in Guatemala—soon nicknamed Happy Valley by the Americans who ran it. There the recruits would be equipped with weapons of World War II vintage and trained by U.S. military personnel. Simultaneously, Cuban exile leaders were urged to unite to form the nucleus of a Cuban government in exile which could be converted into a provisional government when the invasion took place. It was also expected that followers of these exiled Cuban leaders still in Cuba would form an efficient underground movement which might lead a rebellion to coincide with the invasion.

Who were the exiled Cuban leaders? They ranged from former Batista supporters to former Castro supporters who had broken with the revolutionary government. The C.I.A., dimly aware that the Cuban people might not welcome back Batista men, intended to exclude them from the "Revolutionary Council" (as the exile organization was called), but several turned up in the invasion force. Leadership of the Revolutionary Council was given to José Miró Cardona and Antonio de Varona, both of whom had served in the Cuban revolutionary government in the early days after Batista's overthrow, and both of whom had broken with Castro when his reforms seemed to threaten an economic rather than a purely political revolution. There was one group of Cuban exiles who supported most of Castro's economic reforms, such as nationalization of the public utilities and the Agrarian Reform Law, but feared that Castro himself was too weak to prevent a Communist take-over in Cuba. This group, organized as the "People's Revolutionary Movement" and headed by Manuel Ray, was completely excluded from the attempted invasion. It was "too radical" for the C.I.A.'s taste. Yet this was the one group of Cuban exiles who, because they did not represent an attempt to turn back the clock in Cuba, could have counted on some organized support among certain underground elements on the island. But if the C.I.A. did not trust the Manuel Ray group, neither did it trust the conservative group headed by Miró Cardona. Last-minute preparations for the invasion were kept secret from *all* the Cuban exile leaders—and on the day of invasion they were locked up in a Miami motel while the C.I.A. issued in their names communiques over which they had no control!

The basic plan of the invasion worked out by the C.I.A. was this: The Cuban invasion force (which numbered about 1,400 men and called itself the 2506 Brigade after the serial number of recruit Carlos Rodrígues who was killed during training) would land at night, on the southwest coast of Cuba near the *Bahia de Cochinos* (Bay of Pigs). They would be transported from their Guatemalan (and later Nicaraguan) bases in five old boats escorted by two World War II LSTs. Their landing would be protected from Castro's small air force by prior bombing raids carried out by unmarked American B-26 bombers flown by Cuban and American volunteer pilots which would presumably destroy the Cuban air force on the ground. Once ashore, it was expected that the 2506 Brigade would find popular support—at least enough popular support to make its way up into the Escombray Mountains and defend itself from Castro's army for seventy-two hours. It was thought that seventy-two hours would be sufficient to rush over into Cuba a "Cuban provisional government," drawn from the exile groups, which would then formally ask for American aid to help it liberate Cuba. The United States would immediately recognize the provisional government and thus have a legal excuse for direct intervention. An American aircraft carrier and other forces, some based on Guantánamo, would be nearby to land forces when the intervention became legal.

The tactical plan left no room for error. Night was chosen because the element of surprise was crucial; the destruction of Castro's air force, also crucial, was to be accomplished in three raids—no more were to be provided for. The landing area was to be sealed off from Castro's forces by bombing and by the dispatch of a battalion of paratroopers slightly ahead of the seaborne landings. Even on the tactical level, this plan was so unrealistic that the fact of its approval by the Pentagon, which examined it, has led some observers to wonder if the Pentagon, perhaps jealous of its prerogatives, had purposely allowed the plan to go forward as a demonstration that such matters should not be left to C.I.A. "amateurs." A wealth of World War II experience with seaborne invasions had demonstrated that ample margin must be left for error; that nighttime landings were extremely risky because of the possibilities of confusion and misdirection in the dark; that, often as not, paratroopers were dropped far from their objectives; that it was expecting entirely too much to wipe out all of Castro's air force in but three raids by a handful of obsolescent planes; that bombers must have fighter escorts (none had been provided for!) over beachheads; that supplies must be distributed in such a way among transporting ships that the loss of a single vessel would not deprive the invasion forces of vital equipment; that against even moderate resistance at the beachhead, heavy naval gunfire would be required to secure it. Every one of these tactical rules was broken, and disaster ensued.

The decision to actually launch the invasion force was President John F. Kennedy's. He had serious doubts about the wisdom of the entire understaking. Some of his personal advisors opposed it on moral and political grounds. But having been President for but three months, Kennedy felt bound to heed the advice of the "experts" in his State Department, the C.I.A. and the Pentagon. All of these assured him of success—and furthermore that success would lead to a full-scale revolt in Cuba against the "hated" Castro government. Kennedy was in fact as much a prisoner of "expert" ignorance and misinformation as had been his predecessor, President Eisenhower.

The 2506 Brigade set sail from their Nicaraguan and Guatemalan staging areas on April 13, 1961. While still at sea they cheered to hear that Castro's air force had been wiped out on the ground by B-26s in a surprise raid. They were not told that instead of three raids, the B-26s were limited by the American government to but one raid—after Cuban complaints at the United Nations had raised a furor of world opinion that the United States was itself undertaking an invasion of Cuba. As a result only 40% of the Cuban air force had actually been destroyed. The remaining 60% consisted not only of old B-26 bombers, but also of Russian jet fighter-trainer planes which would have no difficulty in coping with the Brigade's own ancient B-26s.

Nor was there any element of surprise in the Brigade's appearance. Cuban spies had long ago reported the training camps and some of the plans to the Cuban revolutionary government. Fidel Castro was well aware that an invasion attempt would be made (indeed his emissaries had never tired of reporting that fact to the United Nations, just as the U.S. State Department never tired of denying it). And on April 16, a preinvasion landing by a small group of 2506 Brigade men who were supposed to guide the main landing was discovered by a Cuban patrol. Shots were exchanged, and Havana was alerted to the precise area where the invaders would land.

Even before the first 2506 Brigade forces were landed (at several points) in the Bay of Pigs area on April 17, the Cuban air force had sunk two of the invasion ships carrying vital supplies. At this, the other ships put out to sea after the landings to avoid being sunk themselves—and out at sea they remained, carrying the Brigade's essential provisions, while the landing forces expended their ammunition. Meanwhile, in several vital areas the paratroopers had been dropped far from their objectives. In any event they lacked the means to close the roads to the beachhead against the rapidly advancing armored forces that Castro now hastily ordered into action. When the Brigade's B-26s attempted to protect the beachhead by bombing, they were shot down by Castro's jet trainers.

While catastrophe engulfed the 2506 Brigade on the beachhead, the American aircraft carrier stationed a few miles outside Cuban territorial waters took no action whatsoever. Despite the frantic appeals of the Brigade, no American jets appeared to protect them (one flight of three jets desperately cheered by the embattled Brigade turned out to be on a photoreconnaissance mission). It was during these hours on April 17 and 18 that Kennedy's "expert" advisors from the C.I.A. and the Pentagon informed him that only American intervention could now save the Brigade. But American intervention was by now politically out of the question. Cuban charges before the United Nations were being proved every minute. And American complicity in the invasion was obvious to the entire world. United States Ambassador to the United Nations Adlai Stevenson, who had been purposely kept in ignorance of the entire Bay of Pigs invasion scheme, hotly denied the Cuban charges at first. But when he realized he'd been trapped into publicly lying by his own government, he fell silent. American intervention now would bring ruin to American influence throughout Latin America and much of the rest of the world—if that influence had not already been irreparably undermined by the crude deceit and harebrained nature of the invasion itself.

The Brigade members fought bravely. When they realized that no air cover would be provided and that their ships would not even attempt to carry them out of the beachhead, they determined to sell their lives dearly. As Castro's armored columns, headed by tanks, crumpled the thin beachhead defenses, the men of the 2506 Brigade were reduced to opposing them with pistols—until their pistol ammunition ran out. Hundreds were killed. A tiny handful made their way through swamps around the beachhead up into the mountains, where they were later captured. Twenty-two put to sea in a small boat (only seven were rescued alive days later), and the rest, 1,113 survivors, surrendered to the Castro forces. In all, they had resisted not for seventy-two hours, but for exactly sixty-two. They had been unable to make their way inland, had never penetrated more than a few miles from the beachhead at most. There had been, of course, no general uprising or even limited rebellion in Cuba itself upon news of the landings. Instead there were huge demonstrations of popular support for Fidel Castro and against an invasion which most Cubans knew was Yankee-backed.

The "politics of ignorance" had cost many brave men their lives; it had caused the United States to suffer a deep and lasting humiliation in the eyes of the entire world; it had ruined American hopes in Latin America and throughout the non-Communist "Third World" of neutralist nations. And, for our purposes of greatest significance, it had now made certain that if Fidel Castro's Cuba had not been Communist before, it would be in the very near future.

10

Slicing the Melon

It is hard to say just when Fidel Castro convinced himself that he was a Communist. One may use the phrase "convinced himself" because to this day he is not accepted as a "serious" Communist by Marxist thinkers or Soviet-bloc politicians. The evidence is scanty as to when this remarkable transformation took place. As early as February 1, 1961, an Italian Communist newspaper published an interview with Castro in which he admitted that Cuban Communists had had reason to distrust his Twenty-Sixth of July Movement because it had been "full of petty bourgeois prejudices and defects." And in Havana on March 25, 1961, at a banquet in honor of the Communist newspaper *Hoy,* he apologized for the fragility of the Twenty-Sixth of July Movement's ideology. In several speeches during 1961 he alluded to his Marxism as if it had always been an accepted fact. In April 1961 he referred to the Cuban Revolution in an offhand way as a "Socialist revolution." But it was not until December 1, 1961, during an hours-long, rambling television speech that Castro declared, "I am a Marxist-Leninist and I will be one until the last day of my life!"

There are many who have insisted that Castro was always a Communist. The dates they suggest for his conversion range from his early youth in high school to the days of training (1955-1956) in Mexico. Their argument runs something like this: Fidel Castro and his closest associates were Communists before they embarked on the Sierra Maestra campaign, certainly before they took power in Havana. But because of the probability of United States intervention against anything that smacked of a real Communist revolution in Cuba, they disguised this fact. During the first two years of their regime, they continued to disguise it, but more and more thinly as time went on, until finally, after the Bay of Pigs invasion, when they had nothing further to lose, they admitted it openly. This argument seems necessary to those who would exculpate the United States from responsibility for events in Cuba. And it is comforting because it fits into the paranoid "secret plot" theory of history cherished by extreme rightists. But if true, this theory must assume that Castro and his followers were able for several years to fool extremely experienced, acute, intelligent and dedicated journalists such as Herbert Matthews of the *New York Times* and Enrique Meneses of *Paris Match* (who lived as close to Castro an anyone could in the Sierra Maestra for months), highly respected outside observers such as Jean Paul Sartre and Ernest Hemingway, and many, many Cubans who split with Castro later *not* because he was a Communist (they considered him definitely *not*) but because he was in danger of *becoming one*. It also overlooks or disregards the testimony of the American C.I.A. which took the trouble to investigate Castro's past intensively.

Although the "plot" theory of Castro's always having been a Communist is a simple way to avoid the hard complexities of what happened in Cuba, it is not necessary to an understanding of Cuban events. Truth is generally more complex than fiction, and so is the truth about Cuba. During the early days of the Castro government, when Twenty-Sixth of July men wanted to taunt the Communists who had failed to support them in the Sierra Maestra and who opposed them in labor union elections they would shout out "*Melon!*" at them. This meant that although the Communists now pretended to be Castroites, they were "green" on the outside (olive-green being the color of the fatigue uniforms of the Twenty-Sixth of July men) but remained "red" on the inside. The deeper they were probed, the redder they would reveal themselves to be. Right or wrong, this accusation or description is more useful if applied to events than to men. The Cuban Revolution itself, green on the outside when it was carried on by Twenty-Sixth of July men, grew redder and redder the deeper it was sliced. But it is not necessary to sink into the quagmire of debating individual viewpoints or beliefs to account for this. There were discernible objective reasons.

First of all, historically speaking, all revolutions become more radical as they progress. The American Revolution was not at first an attempt to win independence from Great Britain, but an attempt by Americans to win what they considered their natural and legal rights *as Englishmen.* It was only after several battles, and several rebuffs from the British government to pacification proposals, that Continental Congress leaders nerved themselves to declare independence their aim. Likewise, the French Revolution progressed from a demand that the king respect the rights of the Estates-General to a demand that the king lose his head. The Russian Revolution passed from the liberal hands of Kerensky and his supporters to the radical hands of the Bolsheviks several months *after* the tsar had been deposed. It may be urged that Sam Adams always wanted independence, that Robespierre always wanted a republic, that Lenin always wanted a Communist state. But to imagine that these individuals simply imposed their will on the broad masses of the people and the complicated rush of events is to misunderstand history. Men make history—and some men may lead others in making it—but just as no man or group of men can produce a revolution where no revolutionary situation exists, so no man or group of men can by themselves force a revolution into more radical paths. Only events impinging on deeply rooted historical movements can do that.

The factors which, again historically speaking, have forced revolutions into more radical paths have been: outside opposition (from Britain in the case of the American Revolution, from the European monarchies in the case of the French Revolution, from the World War I Allied governments in the case of the Russian Revolution); internal

159

opposition (supplied by Tories, aristocrats, the very wealthy, conservative army men, et al.); lack of practical administrative experience among revolutionary leaders (seldom have such leaders understood just how far they would have to go once in power to satisfy the promises and slogans with which they enlisted popular support); and, of very great importance, the fact that measures considered revolutionary "in theory" often turn out in practice to be insufficiently radical to accomplish their ends.

All of these factors were present during the Cuban Revolution. Outside opposition was provided by the United States (and *Batistiano* emigrés); internal opposition was provided by wealthy Cubans, foreign (i.e., U.S.) businessmen and corporate officials, and those sections of the Cuban middle class who feared to oppose them. Lack of practical administrative experience was so widespread as to become something of a standing joke in Cuba. For example, Ché Guevara was named director of the Cuban National Bank, a post for which he was totally unequipped—but, as Herbert Matthews has pointed out, "Castro needed a revolutionary, and there are no revolutionary bankers." And as far as theoretical measures not showing themselves radical enough in practice to achieve their ends, the history of Cuba after Castro's victory abounds in examples, especially if one remembers that one of the primary ends to be achieved was independence from foreign economic domination.

It was found, for example, that simply ordering the Cuban Telephone Company to lower its rates and extend its services was not sufficient; its old owners and managers sabotaged a government program they considered against their interests. Therefore Castro found that his government had to actually take over direct management of the company, and later nationalize it, to accomplish its goals. Under the Agrarian Reform Law it was soon discovered that simply transferring title to the land to peasants did not automatically achieve the desperately necessary end of increasing agricultural output; for that, scientific measures and industrial machinery were necessary. But that in turn presupposed government administration of the land, which could only be carried out through organization. Hence the land which had been "given" to the *guajiros* was almost immediately organized into cooperatives. And when it was found that organizing it into cooperatives did not quickly enough wipe out peasant ignorance of proper farming methods, or provide sufficient tools and manpower to more fully exploit the land, the cooperatives were changed into something approaching collective farms on the Soviet model. It was found that simply passing a law calling upon foreign oil companies to either develop their landholdings or pay heavy taxes on undeveloped land was not sufficient to bring about voluntary development. And first management, then nationalization of these oil companies followed.

Likewise it was found that attempting to defend the revolutionary government against counterrevolutionary attempts by exiles could not be done by purchasing planes and arms from the United States or powers friendly to the United States; therefore those planes and arms would have to come from Communist-bloc nations. Meanwhile the country would have to be defended by mass militia organizations. But militias raised among the people are not professional armies. To keep them in a state of proper discipline and alertness, it is necessary to assure them repeatedly that their revolution and their country are in danger. This leads to overemphasis of the threat of foreign intervention and can degenerate into demagoguery (though in view of what happened, it is hard to see that Castro was "overemphasizing" the threat from abroad). And putting the people into a condition of constant alert, necessary though this may be, increases internal suspicion of "spies," "saboteurs," etc., and can eventually lead to police-state methods of suppressing anyone critical of the regime as a potential enemy of the state and/or the people. An example of this was the hasty arrest of some 100,000 Cubans during the Bay of Pigs invasion—an action applauded by the majority of Cubans. But aside from the fact that this might seem a sensible precaution under the circumstances (much more sensible than the American incarceration of many thousands of innocent American citizens of Japanese descent during World War II), it should be noted that almost all of them were released after the invasion had been turned back.

The objective factors, then, which pushed Castro and other Twenty-Sixth of July leaders into the embrace of the Cuban Communists were: The Communist program of action, both theoretical and

161

practical, increasingly seemed to predict and coincide with an apparently necessary radicalization of the Cuban economy; their experience, both theoretical and practical, increasingly seemed to provide the only source of administrative skills (so badly lacking among Twenty-Sixth of July men) *combined with* a sufficiently radical outlook to make them reliable agents of the Revolution; and, perhaps of greatest importance, the Communist-bloc nations seemed to be the only ones willing to aid the Cuban Revolution economically and protect it militarily. Hence, the Cuban Communists, as representatives of the Soviet bloc, assumed vital significance in Cuba, especially after the Bay of Pigs invasion.

One may add to this certain subjective factors, such as Castro's largely untheoretical background which would hardly equip him to find the fallacies in the monolithic and exceedingly complex structure of Marxist theory, and his decisive and pragmatic personality which would lead him first to suppose that he could "use" Marxism and the Cuban Communists, later that he himself, *el máximo líder,* could develop a "new" Marxism which was more "pragmatic" than the old. Also, Fidel Castro is no more exempt from the ancient maxim that "power corrupts and absolute power corrupts absolutely" than any other man. Lifted dramatically from obscurity to absolute power in Cuba and the attention of the entire world, Castro has tended to identify the Revolution with himself. He is justified in supposing that most Cubans support him, but he has increasingly translated this support into a mystical assumption of union with the Cuban people whereby he need not consult them on many issues—he "knows" what they want because he is Fidel Castro. That this even when true is a very frail reed upon which to support a government has been proved more than once in this century. But it is not necessary to debate the influence of these subjective factors upon the course of Cuban history; objective factors predominate.

In embracing communism, Fidel Castro had to beware of damaging his own image and of undermining his own position. Having denounced the Communists in the past, he had somehow to explain away the old rivalry and enmity between the *Partido Socialista Popular* and the Twenty-Sixth of July Movement. This explains an extraordinary, confusing and intentionally obscure series of speeches, interviews, etc., which he made during 1961. To trace the twistings of this process of rationalizing the past into new forms is profitless. In the end, Castro's ideological confessions seemed satisfactory both to him and to Cuban Communist leaders as a basis for fusion. In the fall of 1961, a new directorate was established to govern Cuba. It consisted of a "fusion" of the leadership of the *Partido Socialista Popular* and the Twenty-Sixth of July Movement, to be called Integrated Revolutionary Organizations (IRO). Supposedly this new directorate included not only Communists and Twenty-Sixth of July men, but also former leaders of the anti-Batista Student Directorate. But this Student Directorate had exercised no real power or influence in Cuba since Castro's triumph, and the only Twenty-Sixth of July men on the IRO council were the two Castro brothers, Ché Guevara, President Dorticós and Emilie Aragonés. All the other members were *Partido Socialista Popular* men. And indeed PSP members had been taking over administrative posts, labor union posts, army command positions, etc., all during the spring and summer of 1961. Blas Roca, a veteran Cuban Communist leader, came to the fore. In August 1961 Roca made a prolonged visit to the Soviet Union, presumably to work out the details of fitting the Cuban economy into complete integration with that of the Communist-bloc countries, and also to discuss plans for Russian defense of Cuba in the event of another Bay of Pigs attempt. It was upon his return that the formation of the IRO was announced.

As far as a Russian contribution to Cuban defense was concerned, this quickly assumed massive proportions. Russian tanks, jet planes, artillery and tactical rockets (ground-to-ground and ground-to-air) poured into Cuba. Along with them came hundreds of Red Army experts to train Cuban soldiers in their use. Long before the Bay of Pigs episode, Soviet Premier Nikita Khrushchev had warned that Russia would defend Cuba with atomic missiles if necessary, but Khrushchev later backed down from that statement, advising that it was meant "only symbolically." Yet the Bay of Pigs invasion, though quickly crushed, had underscored the fact that the United States could, if it so desired, intervene decisively and quickly in Cuba. Khrushchev's boast was revealed as empty. And since the Soviet

Union was in increasing competition with Red China for the allegiance of Communist Parties and countries thoughout the world, Khrushchev's own political position within the world Communist movement was threatened by the weakness of the Soviet defense of Cuba in early 1961. That weakness was soon remedied. It is not yet known exactly when the Soviet government decided to install atomic ballistic missiles in Cuba. But since their installation was not something that could be improvised but required extremely detailed planning well in advance, it seems likely that the decision was made at the time of the Blas Roca visit to Moscow.

But if Russia was to really defend Cuba, and even, as we now know, install aggressive missile systems there, it was extremely important that Fidel Castro and his government demonstrate their reliability and "seriousness" within the world Communist system. On an ideological level this was done during the summer and fall of 1961. It was not done easily or without "backslidings." In early 1962 Castro alarmed Cuban Communists and the Soviet leadership by making several more or less violent attacks on various Communist leaders in Cuba. But these attacks, it soon became clear, were not so much ideological as they were part of Castro's maneuvering to assure himself continuing power within the new Communist-oriented Cuban political system. On an economic level, Cuba proved its Marxist purity by instituting an acceptable Four-Year Plan for the development of the Cuban economy. The Four-Year Plan was a model of Communist bureaucratic planning. It looked forward to a thoroughgoing industrialization of Cuba and a complete rationalization of the Cuban economy. Hundreds of factories were to be erected with Soviet help—and paid for by exports of Cuban sugar. Again, Russian technicans would supervise the factory construction. An estimated four thousand of them arrived during the early months of 1962. Like other such plans, the Cuban Four-Year Plan depended on not only the capital investment of factories and machinery but also the dedication and efficiency of workers. Since the Communists had taken over control of Cuban trade unions, these became the instruments through which worker discipline was to be imposed. And since laxness, absenteeism, and inefficiency were now a matter between the individual worker and the state rather than between workers and private employers, lack of fervor in the factories and cane fields became grounds for suspicion of treason. When the Four-Year Plan showed signs of strain (it was badly adapted to Cuban conditions), when the Cuban economy began crumbling (not only through faults in the Plan, but also for reasons inevitable in the whole scheme of integrating the Cuban economy with that of nations on the other side of the world), charges of "sabotage" became frequent and led to police action. In short, the forced industrialization of Cuba, as it proceeded, began to demand more and more sacrifices from the Cuban people: of their sweat, of their immediate hopes, of their personal liberty. In this, the Communist development in Cuba paralleled Communist development in other sub-industrial states.

An excellent example of the difference between the pre-Communist Cuban Revolution and its Communist phase was its treatment of the press. After Castro's victory, the great Havana daily newspapers such as *La Marina, Hoy, Bohemia* and others, representing viewpoints across the political spectrum from conservative Catholicism to communism, continued to publish and to voice their opinions without hindrance. During 1959 and 1960 and even 1961 they printed criticisms of Fidel Castro and his movement and the entire Cuban Revolutionary government. But they did this in a revolutionary atmosphere, and that atmosphere imposed its own hindrances. For example, linotypists and pressmen as well as reporters habitually appended footnotes to articles or editorials in their newpapers which expressed the viewpoint of the owners in opposition to their own. In these footnotes they would argue against the content or style of a particular report or editorial. Newspaper owners complained that this was an unheard-of infringement upon their right, but if it was, it was a revolutionary expansion of the right of newspaper workers to be effectively heard. As the Revolution grew older, increasingly there were instances of newspaper workers' committees trying to turn the tables and dictate to management what kind of news and views their newspapers should present. On occasion such committees actually seized newspaper offices and plants. This was certainly interference with freedom of the press. But it was interference from below, not interference imposed by the government. In many cases it was due only to government intervention that newspapers were *not* taken over by such committees. There was no government censorship of news, nor was there any government restriction on the free circulation of newspapers and magazines from the United States and elsewhere. The successive closing down of independent newspapers in Havana until mid-1961 was due to economic factors in almost every case. That these economic (and social, for it must not be forgotten that angry workers' committees could very well frighten editorialists and owners) factors were the result of the Revolution, was undeniable. That the Cuban revolutionary government was not going to seriously curb revolutionary activities and enthusiasms for the benefit of newspaper publishers was also obvious. In this sense, but only in this sense, it may be argued that the Cuban Revolution curtailed press freedom from the beginning. But if newspaper publishers and foreign observers thought the Revolution had gone too far in this direction, they found out what a true press censorship could be like after Castro's merger with the Cuban Communist movement. All the usual blundering, clumsy apparatus of official government press censorship then descended, and Havana's newspapers began to disappear. By 1962 government control of the press was as absolute in Cuba as it was in Russia.

But Cuba's turn toward Communism was modified by several inescapable factors: that American power was predominant and only sixty miles away; that trade with the United States and other Western nations would, on a purely economic and financial basis, better meet Cuba's needs than trade with distant Communist nations; that the entire cultural climate of Cuba was perhaps unsuited to disciplined bureaucracy of any kind at all. As to this last, no one really knew. Cuba was the first Spanish-speaking, nominally Catholic, Latin-cultured subtropical land to undertake the Communist experiment. Cuban variations noticeable in theoretical and practical communism, and often ascribed to Castro's personality, might perhaps better be ascribed to Cuba's unique culture within the Communist orbit.

As to Castro's continuing impact on events, this was not to be discounted. It was dramatically illustrated by his treatment of the 1,100 prisoners taken from the 2506 Brigade during the abortive Bay of

Pigs fiasco. When they had been rounded up and taken off to Havana, Castro himself confronted them in the Confederation of Labor Hall in a memorable interview that was televised throughout Cuba. As Castro himself pointed out, these proceedings presented "the unique spectacle of a government head conducting a public discussion with prisoners who came to overthrow him."

Guarding the prisoners were armed militiamen who kept breaking into the "debate" with shouts of *"Paredon!"* ("To the wall!"—that is, let's line them up and shoot them all.) When Castro implied that the 2506 Brigade had been nothing but mercenaries, the prisoners angrily shouted denials. One of them declared: "Sir, I came to combat communism; to have elections; to uphold the Constitution of 1940, free enterprise and the rights of citizens."

When one of the prisoners asked Castro if the Cuban government was Communist (remember, this was in April 1961), Castro replied: "If the people of Cuba want a Communist regime, who has the right to deny it to them?" He said, however, that the Cuban government had some Socialist, some non-Socialist elements in it. Finally, despite the continuing shouts of *"Paredon!"* Castro announced that clemency would be shown and that prisoners would not be executed (they were, formally, traitors and could well have suffered the death penalty).

If this public spectacle was unique, unique too was Castro's proposal that if the United States wished to have these men returned, then the Americans should pay, in medical supplies, machinery, etc., the equivalent of the dollar value of the damage done by the invasion. The U.S. government refused to officially take part in what it considered the payment of "ransom." But the Kennedy administration made certain that the "private" efforts of a group headed by James B. Donovan, lawyer and former head of World War II's office of Strategic Services, were successful. Negotiations over the prisoners were agonizingly protracted, lasting for nearly two years. Meanwhile, the men were kept in the same prison on the Isle of Pines in which Castro himself had been held after the failure of the Moncada Barracks attack. Conditions were rigorous, much harsher than those Castro had himself suffered. But none of the prisoners was tortured and none died as a result of their captivity. When they were finally released and flown back to Miami on the day before Christmas, 1962, many of them were fit and willing enough to accept the U.S. government's offer of enlisting in the armed forces.

But by that time Fidel Castro may well have felt he could afford to exercise clemency. His revolution was now so well armed and equipped by the Soviet Union that no possible combination of exiled Cuban groups could hope to successfully raid or invade Cuba again. If Castro was to be overthrown from outside, that overthrow would have to be nothing less than a full-scale American military intervention. But that was a very remote possibility after the events of October 1962. For it will be recalled that it was in October 1962, that American reconnaissance planes began taking a very close look at certain Russian installations in Cuba. It was on the 22nd of October that it was announced that President Kennedy would address the United States (and the world) at seven o'clock that evening on television. . . .

Assessing the Revolution

Perhaps one should ask first: Was it a real revolution? Yes, it was. It shifted power from one class to another; it definitely wrested state and economic power from the hands of the Cuban middle classes, the owners of the means of production (of land, sugar mills, factories, mines, rentable properties, etc.), and gave that power into the hands of a group who claimed to represent the Cuban lower classes, the workers and *guajiros*. It also effectively eliminated foreign ownership of the means of production and replaced it with Cuban. But the limitations on the extent of this transfer of power were quickly expressed. These limitations have to do with the question of whether or not the Cuban workers and *guajiros* actually received and retained the power for which they had struggled. This power is not to be confused with "benefits," no matter how eagerly received or widespread. It has to do with real political and economic control of Cuban means of production. Like so much else in recent Cuban history, the answer to this question is ambivalent and depends largely on who answers it.

169

The Cuban government, which, like other Soviet-style regimes, administers and controls all sectors of the nation's economy, would reply that since they are the people's representatives and enjoy the support of the overwhelming majority of the Cuban people, their exercise of power is the people's exercise of power. But since the Cuban government, like other Soviet-style regimes, has no means of determining the popular will in any formal sense (elections being uncontested in any meaningful way), this claim must remain just that—a claim. Objectively speaking, it must be said that decisive power in Cuba today rests in the hands of Fidel Castro, the Cuban Communist Party, and the Cuban governmental bureaucracy. These may seek to identify themselves with the popular will, but it must be remembered that all bureaucrats are men, and all men are human. The administration of power by any bureaucracy, whether corporate or state, and especially one over which the people exercise no formal control, must be assumed to be at least potentially dictatorial. In that sense it may be said that although the Cuban Revolution transferred power from the owning classes to the working and peasant classes at first, the erection of a Communist government there has removed that power once again—into the hands of the government itself, which may or may not exercise it in accordance with the popular will. Therefore it seems safe to say that the Cuban Revolution achieved its primary aim, but only with important limitations.

What of the elimination of foreign ownership of Cuban means of production? Here again the answer is at best ambivalent. United States ownership has certainly been completely eliminated, and no other foreign ownership has come to replace it in a formal sense. But where ownership is in the hands of the state itself, then it is fair to ask if the state itself is not partly dominated by foreign interests. Cuba is certainly sovereign and independent. But its heavy reliance on Soviet-bloc trade and assistance makes it, partly at any rate, a dependency of the Communist family of nations. It must sell its produce largely to that block, at prices determined not by Cuba or by the vagaries of free economics, but by Soviet block governments. It must also purchase manufactured goods and oil, etc., from the Soviet bloc, again at prices imposed by that bloc's leaders. Recent outspoken

170

criticism of Russian foreign policy is made within the framework of continued economic dependence, although after the missile crisis Castro turned increasingly toward Red China for trade and aid. Thus the slight "room for maneuver" which Cuba can exercise in its present economic-political foreign policy is that provided by the rift between the Soviet Union and Red China. But this room is narrow precisely because Cuba is of no very great economic, political or even strategic value to either of the Communist colossi.

This hard fact of international life was brought vividly home to Fidel Castro during the Cuban missile crisis. Soviet Premier Nikita Khrushchev did not bother to consult Castro during his frenzied negotiations with Kennedy. He did not consult him when he decided to remove the Cuban-based missiles, nor when he accepted Kennedy's conditional pledge not to invade Cuba if the missiles *were* removed. Nor was Castro consulted by Khrushchev when he accepted on-site inspection by United Nations teams of the former missile sites, even though such inspection would have to be made on Cuban territory. Castro demonstrated his irritation with all this by flatly refusing to permit UN inspection teams into Cuba, despite a hurried visit by Anastas Mikoyan. And since that inspection was never carried out (U.S. reconnaissance planes made sure of the missile sites' dismantling), as President Kennedy pointed out, the United States commitment not to invade Cuba remained conditional. Yet within the overall structure of world power and politics, such an invasion was the remotest possibility.

It would not long remain "remote," however, if Cuba undertook any large-scale attempts at subverting the precarious structure of Latin American relations with the United States. Not that these relations needed any outside impulse to continue to deteriorate. It appeared that the United States had learned but little from its experiences with Cuba. Kennedy's "Alliance for Progress" and other aid programs showed a modest American effort to reform some of the institutions and better the economic life of South American countries before these too exploded into revolution. But this effort was much too small, and was continually hampered by the demands of American business investors and corporations holding properties in these countries. It was also misdirected in the sense that it continued to rely often on discredited political leaders and be manipulated by conscienceless elements of South America's economic ruling oligarchy. And how blundering the U.S. State Department could be in its handling of Latin American affairs was once again demonstrated under the administration of President Lyndon B. Johnson by the ill-advised, hasty and fear-inspired intervention of U.S. Marines in the troubled post-Trujillo Dominican Republic.

It was to circumvent possible American retribution on Cuba that when Ché Guevara decided the time was ripe for him to lead another revolutionary guerrilla war—this time in Bolivia—he formally renounced his ties to the Cuban government and even his (honorary) Cuban citizenship. As we have seen, Ché was always convinced that all of South America would one day have to throw off the Yankee "yoke." His activities in Cuba had always been, to him, only a stepping-stone toward a wider, perhaps continent-wide, revolution. During the second week of October 1965, Fidel Castro announced the departure of Ché Guevara by reading to a gathering of five thousand Cubans Ché's farewell letter: "I believe I have now carried out my mission in the Cuban Revolution. I bid farewell to you, to our comrades. . . . Other parts of the world need the help of my modest efforts, and the moment has arrived for us to part." The outcome of Ché's tragically misdirected guerrilla war in the mountains and forests of Bolivia, where he attempted to recreate the same sort of revolutionary movement which had won in Cuba under totally different conditions, is well known. His small band of followers was reduced to a mere handful by constant battles, desertions and exhaustion. Ché himself was captured by special units of the Bolivian army (which had been trained and equipped in the United States) on October 8, 1967, after being wounded in his last engagement. He was executed without trial (that is to say, murdered) the following day, October 9, by his captors, precisely because they feared the impact his eloquence might have at a formal trial. In murdering him the Bolivian army only succeeded in adding a particularly bright legend to the pantheon of Latin American revolutionary martyrs.

And what of the people of Cuba, of the workers and *guajiros* for whom and through whom the Revolution was fought and won? There can be little doubt that most Cubans are better off in many ways today than they have ever been before. Education has all but removed the blight of illiteracy from the Cuban countryside; *guajiros* can read and write now and their children are able to attend decent schools and even the university. Government medical aid in the form of new hospitals and squads of doctors sent out into the countryside have also wrought tremendous changes for the better in *guajiro* life. Furthermore, the general national program of improving roads and communications has largely eliminated the isolation in which Cuba's peasants used to live. For the city workers, the government's efforts to create new housing and to rationalize the old have been of great importance, as have been price controls, improved social-security benefits and assured employment. The moral climate of Cuba has also undergone a radical change. Prostitutes no longer crowd Havana's streets; gangsters no longer dominate Havana's nightlife. The beaches, hotels and places of recreation in the capital are now open to (and within the reach of) all Cubans.

But despite all this, many Cubans remained dissatisfied. They remained dissatisfied enough to flee by the thousands when given the opportunity. They were given the opportunity on September 28, 1965, when during a speech, Fidel Castro stated that any Cuban who wished to leave Cuba could do so without molestation by the Cuban government. In the weeks and months that followed, some 200,000 Cubans fled—mostly to the United States. Combined with Cubans who had left Cuba before that offer, that made a grand total of some 300,000 Cubans in voluntary or enforced exile—5% of the total population! Nor could it be claimed that all of these were *Batistianos* or "the rich" or "counterrevolutionaries;" the numbers were too great to be accounted for in that way. Without doubt very many of the fleeing Cubans were simply people who could not stand the rigors of enforced industrialization and rationalization of the Cuban economy, with all its attendant shortages and wastages and discipline. Nonetheless, this "exodus," with Cuban government approval, was another token of how Fidel Castro's regime differed from "normal" Communist governments—as a comparison between the free exit of Cubans in 1965 and the Berlin Wall which kept East Germans prisoners within their own country would indicate.

For the most part, most Cubans today continue to support Fidel Castro and, however grudgingly, the Communist regime he heads. If questioned about such matters as personal liberty and political freedom, most Cubans, who have never really known either, would reply that now they eat, are fairly decently housed, receive an education, benefit from economic security even if on a relatively low level. Furthermore, they are aware that they have broken Yankee domination of Cuban affairs. But above all, right or wrong, the Cuban people live in great hopes for the future. They feel that at long last they control their own destiny, even if they must precariously balance between Communist-bloc (either Russian or Chinese) influence and American suspicions, and that therefore everything is possible. Whether the future they dream of will somehow find a way to reconcile a socialist economy with free political institutions, whether Cuba can find some way out of the international corner it has been forced into by United States and Soviet imperialisms, whether state economic power can be prevented from developing into a ponderous bureaucracy—all of this cannot be foreseen. But in Cuba, at least, solutions to these problems are being actively sought. And if Fidel Castro's revolution has taught the world anything, it is that determined, dedicated men, provided they truly express the popular will, can have a deep impact on the course of history. Miracles, it would seem, can still be accomplished, and a handful of men can defeat armies and defy the powers of this world.

174

BIBLIOGRAPHY
(A "Recommended Reading" list will be found at the end of the Bibliography.)

ALEXANDER, R.J., *Communism in Latin America,* New Brunswick: 1957.

BATISTA, FULGENCIO, *Respuesta,* Mexico City: 1961.

BRENNAN, RAY, *Castro, Cuba, and Justice,* Garden City: 1959.

BUELL, RAYMOND L., *Cuba and the Platt Amendment,* New York: 1929.

CASTRO, FIDEL, *Pensamiento Político, Económico y Social de Fidel Castro,* Havana: 1959.

CASUSO, TERESA, *Cuba and Castro,* New York: 1961.

CHADWICK, FRENCH E., *The Relations of the United States and Spain* (3 vols.), New York: 1911.

CHAPMAN, CHARLES E., *A History of the Cuban Republic,* New York: 1927.

DRAPER, THEODORE, *Castroism: Theory and Practice,* New York: 1962.

DRAPER, THEODORE, *Castro's Revolution: Myths and Realities,* New York: 1962.

DuBOIS, JULES, *Fidel Castro—Rebel Liberator or Dictator?,* New York: 1959.

ENGLER, ROBERT, *The Politics of Oil,* New York: 1961.

FRANK, WALDO, *Cuba: Prophetic Island,* New York: 1962.

GUEVARA, ERNESTO, *The Complete Bolivian Diaries of Ché Guevara* (trans. by Daniel James), New York: 1968.

GUEVARA, ERNESTO, *On Guerrilla Warfare,* New York: 1961.

GUEVARA, ERNESTO, *Reminiscences of the Cuban Revolutionary War* (trans. by Victoria Ortiz), New York: 1968.

HILL, HOWARD C., *Roosevelt and the Caribbean,* Chicago: 1927.

HUBERMAN, LEO, AND SWEEZY, PAUL M., *Cuba, Anatomy of a Revolution,* New York: 1960.

INTERNATIONAL BANK FOR RECONSTRUCTION AND DEVELOPMENT, *Report on Cuba,* Baltimore: 1951.

JENKS, LELAND, *Our Cuban Colony*, New York: 1929.

JIMÉNEZ, ANTONIO NÚÑEZ, *Geografía de Cuba*, Havana: 1954.

JONES, CHESTER LLOYD, *The Caribbean Since 1900*, New York: 1936.

LIEUWEN, EDWIN, *Arms and Politics in Latin America*, New York: 1960.

MATTHEWS, HERBERT L., *The Cuban Story*, New York: 1961.

MENESES, ENRIQUE, *Fidel Castro* (trans, by J. Halcro Ferguson), New York: 1966.

MILLIS, WALTER, *The Martial Spirit*, New York: 1925.

MILLS, C. WRIGHT, *Listen, Yankee!*, New York: 1960.

NELSON, LOWRY, *Rural Cuba*, Minneapolis: 1950.

PEDRERO, ENRIQUE GONZÁLEZ, *La Revolución Cubana*, Mexico City: 1959.

PHILLIPS, RUBY HART, *Cuba: Island of Paradox*, New York: 1959.

SARTRE, JEAN PAUL, *Sartre et Cuba*, Paris: 1959.

SMITH, EARL T., *The Fourth Floor*, New York: 1962.

SMITH, ROBERT F., *The United States and Cuba: Business and Diplomacy, 1917-1960*. New Haven: 1960.

STOKES, WILLIAM S., *Latin American Politics*, New York: 1959.

TABER, ROBERT, *M-26: Biography of a Revolution*, New York: 1961.

UNITED STATES DEPARTMENT OF COMMERCE, *Investment in Cuba*, Washington: 1956.

UNITED STATES DEPARTMENT OF STATE, *Cuba* (White Paper), Washington: 1961.

UNITED STATES SENATE, *Hearings Before the Senate Internal Security Subcommittee, 86th Cong., 2nd sess.*, Washington: 1960.

WEYL, NATHANIEL, *Red Star Over Cuba*, New York: 1960.

ZEITLIN, MAURICE, AND SCHEER, ROBERT, *Cuba: Tragedy in Our Hemisphere*, New York: 1963.

Recommended Reading:

DRAPER, THEODORE, *Castro's Revolution, Myths and Realities*, New York: 1962. (An anti-Castro analysis with emphasis on Cuba's "two revolutions.")

GUEVARA, ERNESTO, *The Complete Bolivian Diaries of Ché Guevara* (trans. by Daniel James), New York: 1968. (Exciting, deeply moving story of a guerrilla campaign that failed.)

GUEVARA, ERNESTO, *Reminiscences of the Cuban Revolutionary War* (trans. by Victoria Ortiz), New York: 1968.
(The only detailed, fairly complete account of the Sierra Maestra campaign, by a man who was an excellent prose stylist as well as a revolutionary.)

MENESES, ENRIQUE, *Fidel Castro* (trans, by J. Halcro Ferguson), New York: 1966.
(A Spanish journalist with Castro in the Sierra Maestra, who happened to be present at most of the important events described in this book.)

MILLIS, WALTER, *The Martial Spirit,* New York: 1925.
(The wittiest account of American intervention in Cuba from 1822 to 1902, with emphasis on the Spanish-American War.)

ZEITLIN, MAURICE, AND SCHEER, ROBERT, *Cuba: Tragedy in Our Hemisphere,* New York: 1963.
(Extremely well-documented, generally sympathetic account of the Cuban Revolution by two men who have studied it deeply.)

Index

*Italic page numbers indicate illustrations.